The Thracian City of Seuthopolis

Dimitur P. Dimitrov and Maria Čičikova

translated from the Bulgarian by
Marguerite P. Alexieva

BAR Supplementary Series 38
1978

British Archaeological Reports

122, Banbury Road, Oxford OX2 7BP, England

GENERAL EDITORS

A. C. C. Brodribb, M.A.
Mrs. Y. M. Hands

A. R. Hands, B.Sc., M.A., D.Phil.
D. R. Walker, M.A.

B.A.R. Supplementary Series 38, 1978: "The Thracian City of Seuthopolis."
© Dimitur P. Dimitrov and Maria Čičikova, c/o Jusautor, Sofia, Bulgaria,
1978.

ISBN 9780860540038 paperback
ISBN 9781407346670 e-book
DOI https://doi.org/10.30861/9780860540038
A catalogue record for this book is available from the British Library

This book is available at www.barpublishing.com

CONTENTS

**Please note that additional material is available to download from
www.barpublishing.com/additional-downloads.html.
The original foldout has been reduced in size to match the A4 format of this book,
the image is therefore not as clear as the original foldout. Please refer to the original
foldout via the download for the original content.**

LIST OF ABBREVIATIONS

AAPhil Acta Antiqua Philippopolitana.

AGSP Antichnie goroda Severnogo Prichernomoriya
(Ancient cities of North Black Sea Shore).

BCH Bulletin de Correspondance Hellénique.

BSA Annual of the British School of Athens.

GNAMPI Godishnik na Narodniya archeologicheski
Muzei Plovdiv.
(Year Book of the National Archaeological
Museum in Plovdiv).

GSOu IFF Godishnik na Sofiiskiya Oouniversitet,
Istorico-filologicheski fakultet.
(Year Book of the University of Sofia,
Department of History and Philology).

IAI Izvestiya na Arheologicheskiya Institut (Sofia).
(Bulletin of the Archaeological Institute).

MCA Materiale şi cercetări arheologice (Bucareşti).
(Materials and Archaeological Researches).

SA Sovetskaya Arheologiya (Moscow).

SCIV Studii şi cercetări de istorie veche
(Bucareşti).
(Studies and Researches of Ancient History).

VDI Vestnik drevnej istorii (Moscow).

PREFACE

The discovery of the Thracian city of Seuthopolis is the most important achievement of Thracian archaeology in the last 30 years in Bulgaria. The city was discovered during the digging undertaken in connection with the construction of the large Georgi Dimitrov Dam on the River Toundja, the ancient Tonsos, 8 km west of the modern town of Kazanluk. The very first sods turned in the basin of the dam reservoir led to the organizing on a large scale of archaeological excavations by the Archaeological Institute and Museum at the Bulgarian Academy of Sciences. A numerous group of research fellows and technical assistants, under the guidance of corresponding member of the Academy Prof. Dimiter P. Dimitrov, who was Director of the Archaeological Museum in Sofia at that time, worked at these excavations with persistence and self-denial for 7 years, from 1948 to 1954. The discoveries made in the course of digging were unexpected. The expedition came upon the ruins of a Thracian city which was almost completely revealed. The name of the city — Seuthopolis — was established, the capital of Seuthes III, a Thracian ruler of the Early Hellenistic epoch, a city previously unknown to history.

Besides the head of the expedition, Prof. D. P. Dimitrov, the members of the group were: Maria Čičikova, deputy head of the dig, Lyuba Ognenova-Marinova, Anna Alexieva-Balkanska and Yordanka Changova, research fellows of the Archaeological Institute at the Bulgarian Academy of Sciences, Gergana Tabakova-Tsanova, curator at the Iskra Museum in Kazanluk, and Dimiter Nikolov of the Historical Museum in the town of Stara Zagora. A large number of students of history and architecture also took part in the digging, doing their practical work here. The plans were made by architect Detelin Moushev and architect Kosta Chervenrakov, the drawings of the altar-hearths were the work of Lyuba Ognenova and architect Nikolai Gyulbarov. The photographs of the terrain were made by Prof. D. P. Dimitrov, and of the finds by Rosa Staneva, head of the Photo Studio at the Archaeological Museum in Sofia. We express our warm thanks to all for their collaboration and assistance during the diggings, and also in preparing the present publication.

There is already an extensive literature on Seuthopolis, one which includes preliminary reports, as well as special studies on important questions concerning the economic and cultural development of the city. Unfortunately the premature death of Academician Prof. D. P. Dimitrov did not allow him to finish his studies of Seuthopolis and to see the complete publication of the results, a work on the preparation of which he and the group who took part in the diggings were engaged at the time of his death. However, the work is to continue, the authors being guided in their research by the valuable instructions of their head and beloved teacher.

The present book includes the studies of Academician D. P. Dimitrov on The Town-Planning and Architecture of Seuthopolis — Chapter I, and on The Thracian Religion on the Basis of Epigraphic Data — Chapter IV, 1 and the Conclusion.

The Introduction, Chapter II — Economic Life and Chapter IV, 2, 3 — Cult Hearths and Funeral Customs — are the work of Maria Čičikova.

Kamen Dimitrov is the author of Chapter III — Monetary Circulation and the Mint of Seuthes III. He wrote this summarizing review on the basis of the catalogue partly composed, but left unfinished by D. P. Dimitrov.

Maria Čičikova

INTRODUCTION

In Antiquity the central and the Eastern part of the Balkan Peninsula was inhabited by the Thracians, a prolific branch of the Indo-European family. Ancient Greek mythology and written tradition have preserved many memories of them. Homer was already familiar with 'the snowy Thracian mountains with the highest peaks' and the Thracian land, 'mother of sheep and home of swift horses'. Hecataeus of Miletus mentions Thracian settlements in the interior of the country situated at the foot of the Haemus (the Balkan Range) and along the banks of the Danube. From the fifth century B.C. onwards data about the Thracians begin to be more frequent. The Thracian coasts of the Black Sea, the Sea of Marmara and the Aegean had at that time been finally occupied by the Greek colonists who founded a number of flourishing colonies, such as Tomi (today Constanţa), Odessos (Varna), Mesambria (Nessebur), Apollonia (Sozopol), Byzantion (Istanbul) on the Black Sea, Perinthus on the Sea of Marmara, Aenus, Abdera and Amphipolis on the Aegean. Thrace was included in the range of the economy of the Eastern Mediterranean world and closely involved in the historical events which took place in this part of the antique world in the second half of the first millennium B.C. The history of the Thracians in this period is to be found in the works of Herodotus, Thucydides, Xenophon, Diodorus, Strabo and other ancient authors in whom we find valuable data on Thracian culture, religion and customs.[1] They also give us the names of many Thracian tribes, the most important of which were the Odrysae, who inhabited the fertile valleys along the lower reaches of the Tonsos (Toundja) and the Hebros (Maritsa), together with the region of the Eastern Rhodopes. In the early years of the fifth century B.C. the Odrysae had already succeeded in creating a large state, whose territory from the end of the fifth to the early third century B.C. also included the middle and the upper reaches of the River Toundja. The considerable archaeological discoveries in the regions of Stara Zagora, Sliven, Yambol and Svilengrad are of great importance in recreating the cultural and political history of the Odrysae. This was the only Thracian state which existed for a comparatively lengthy time and played an important role in the life of the Southern Thracian lands in the period from the end of the fifth to the end of the fourth century B.C. After the death of Kotys I in 359 B.C. the centrifugal forces in the Odrysaean kingdom got the upper hand and it was divided into three parts, which contributed to its political and economic weakening. This facilitated the aspirations of Philip II, who undertook the subjection of Thrace to secure his rear before the decisive engagement with Athens. In several campaigns he succeeded in crushing the resistance of the Thracians, headed by Kersebleptes, and in about 342-339 included Thrace within the boundaries of the Macedonian Kingdom.[2] It would appear, however, that neither Philip nor Alexander succeeded in lastingly subjecting the Thracian Hinterland. The Macedonian presence was chiefly concentrated in Aegean Thrace and along the Rivers Toundja and Maritsa, where Macedonian garrisons were left. The unsubmissive tribal chieftains were probably replaced, but nevertheless certain of the local dynasts were left at the head of individual Thracian tribes. It is quite possible that Seuthes occupied such a position, of which he made skilful use to place himself at the head of the struggles of his fellow-tribesmen against the Macedonian invaders.[3] In a Decree issued by the Athenian Assembly in 331-330 B.C. mention is made of 'Rhebulas, son of Seuthes and brother of Kotys'. The political situation gives grounds to link the Seuthes mentioned in this decree with Seuthes III, who had tried to restore the traditional Odrysaean-Athenian relations, depending on Athens in his struggle against the Macedonians.[4] The reason for this rapprochement with Athens was the mutiny which broke out at the same time (331 B.C.) headed by Memnon, one of Alexander's most capable strategoi, left in Thrace to strengthen Macedonian rule. However, Memnon betrayed Alexander, decided to break away from the King and to become the independent ruler of Thrace. He stirred the 'barbarians' to revolt and organized a great anti-Macedonian rebellion.[5] The rebellion in Thrace intensified the anti-Macedonian moods in Greece as well, at the head of which stood the Spartan King Agis III. Antipater swiftly put down both rebellions. However, this did not put an end to the struggles of the Thracians against the Macedonians, and their revolts followed one another in rapid succession. The failure of Zopyrion's expedition against the Getae, the Scythians and the Pontic cities in 329-328 B.C., and the news of the doom of Alexander's commander at Olbia served as a signal to Seuthes III to intensify his actions.[6] He appears to have achieved considerable success and his kingdom grew rapidly stronger.

The following data about Seuthes go back to the year 323 B.C. After the death of Alexander Thrace was established as an individual Satrapy and given to Lysimachus. He clashed with Seuthes III on his arrival in Thrace, the Thracian king leading out against him 20,000 foot and 8,000 horse.[7] He does not appear to have allowed Lysimachus to establish military control over the interior of the country. The power of Lysimachus over the Thracian Hinterland appears to have been only nominal. His presence in Thrace was limited chiefly to the coastal strip of the Pontus and to Thracian Chersonese.[8] The severity of his clashes with Seuthes can be judged by the fact that he was unable to intervene in the Lamian War (323-322) and to come to Antipater's aid, although he was nearest to the theatre of military operations.[9] On the other hand, the flourishing of Seuthes' city after 323 shows that he had secured the independence of the territories he controlled. It may be no accident that as early as 323 and 313 Diodorus calls Seuthes 'King of the Thracians'.

Seuthes also intervened in the third war which broke out among the Diadochi in 315 B.C., in their struggles to divide Alexander's heritage. Lysimachus, Cassander, Seleucus and Ptolemy organized a strong coalition against the aggression of Antigonus the One-Eyed, governor of Great Phrygia, who, however, took decisive steps against them by transporting his troops to the European shore, getting in touch with the Greek cities on the Black Sea coast and the Thracians of the Hinterland, headed by Seuthes, and promising them his support in their resistance against Lysimachus. In 313 B.C. when the rebellion of Callatis broke out common military operations concerted between the Greek cities, the Odrysae and Antigonus began, the latter sending his commander Lyconos with a fleet into the Pontus, and Pausanias with troops into Thracian Chersonese.[10] Lysimachus succeeded in capturing Odessos and organizing the siege of Callatis, but was forced to march south swiftly to meet Pausanias. However, Seuthes III had already taken over the passes in the Balkan Range and barred his road back. A bloody battle was fought between the two. This is how Diodorus describes it :[11] 'When Lysimachus with the best part of his troops arrived at the watershed of the Haemus, he found there the Thracian King Seuthes who was guarding the pass with many soldiers. After waging battle with him for quite a long time, and losing not a few of his men, he slew many of the enemy and repelled the barbarians. ' Lysimachus succeeded in breaking his way through (quite possibly after an agreement with Seuthes) and defeating Pausanias. Seuthes is not mentioned again in the sources. Until recently the explanation was accepted that he recognized the rule of Lysimachus and fully submitted to him, or fled to his ally Antigonus.[12] Recently the supposition has been put forward that at the end of the fourth century B.C. Lysimachus sought an understanding with Seuthes III, in order to direct his forces to Asia Minor, where severe trials awaited him.[13] The scanty data available in written tradition about this important and dramatic period in the history of Southern Thrace were richly supplemented by the discovery of Seuthopolis.[14] The study of the capital of Seuthes III, which acquired its greatest prosperity and importance in the last decades of the fourth century and the first decades of the third century B.C., eloquently shows that Seuthes had succeeded in founding the independent Odrysaean Kingdom along the upper reaches of the Toundja in the region between the Balkan Range and the Sredna Gora Mountains, and following the example of the other Hellenistic rulers, he had built a capital to which he gave his own name, Seuthopolis (Fig. 1). Moreover, the coins of Cassander and Lysimachus with the title βασιλεύς which Seuthes overstruck, are proof that he struck coins even after 306 B.C. and also that he played a foremost part in Thrace until the end of the fourth century B.C.[15] The great inscription found in Seuthopolis offers us the last information about Seuthes III. The inscription can be dated to the very end of the fourth or the beginning of the third century B.C. when Seuthes was seriously ill or already dead, as can be concluded from the text. Berenice, the Regent, was at the head of affairs in Seuthopolis. If in the decree from Athens (331-330 B.C.) Rhebulas and Kotys, are really the sons of Seuthes III, then Berenice was the second wife of Seuthes III,[16] and was probably a princess of Macedonian origin. She bore Seuthes four sons, Hebriselmes, Teres, Satokos and Sadallas, with names characteristic of the Thracian Royal Family who, at the end of the fourth century, were not yet of age. The inscription is a sworn treaty of Berenice and her sons as regards Epimenes. This name is met with for the first time and it is not clear who Epimenes was and what position he occupied. Nevertheless, he was an eminent personage who had taken refuge in the Sanctuary of the Great Gods in the palace of Seuthopolis, and according to the treaty he was to be handed over to Spartokos to serve him all his life. It is clear from the interpretation of the text that Spartokos was a Thracian dynast whose residence was in Kabyle, a Thracian city to the East of Seuthopolis at the bend of the River Toundja. He was an independent master of a Thracian dynastic estate on the territory or in the neighbourhood of Seuthes' kingdom, which is a sign of the intensified process of political decentralization in Thrace after the death of Seuthes III, a process which was further intensified after the Celtic invasion of the Balkans (280-277).

CHAPTER I

TOWN-PLANNING AND ARCHITECTURE

The place where the ruins of the Thracian city of Seuthopolis were discovered lies about 8 km to the west of the town of Kazanluk and about 3 km
to the south-west of the village of Koprinka. Here, owing to the erosion of
the River Toundja (the ancient Tonsos), a wide terrace-like place had been
formed, bound on the north and east by the gradually sloping plateau, and on
the south by steep heights, sloping to the banks of the river, these heights
being part of the last foothills of the Sredna Gora Mountains. The last and
lowest step of this terrace-like locality on the south-west and the south is
cut by the bends of the Toundja, while on the east by its small tributary
Golyama Varovitsa. In this way a peninsula was formed with banks on the
river up to 4-5 m in height. This is where the Thracian city of Seuthopolis
was situated, on the left bank of the Toundja, naturally protected on the south-
west, the south and the east (Fig. 2).

Until excavations were begun in 1948 no one knew about the existence of
this city. Its name was not met with in a single ancient source. Nevertheless, the traces of antique culture in these places had not been entirely effaced
by time and men. The large number of tumuli scattered in several groups
on both sides of the river had already impressed travellers in the last century.

The construction of the large Georgi Dimitrov Dam was begun in 1947,
and its artificial lake was to cover this entire locality with its waters. This
led to the Archaeological Institute and Museum at the Bulgarian Academy of
Sciences in Sofia organizing the archaeological study of the site. Digging
began in 1948 and continued until 1954. Two of the large tumuli in which
several tombs were found were excavated in the first two seasons. The
boundaries of the settlement with its fort, part of the towers and two of the
city gates were established as early as 1948. Work inside the settlement
began in 1950. Year by year the finds grew more and more varied and interesting. In the first diggings individual buildings, streets, wells, pottery
— Thracian and Greek — terracottas, etc., came to light. The finds of coins
were particularly numerous. Over 2,000 coins were found of which 1,200
were fourth to third century B.C. and the remainder were dated to the 13th-
14th century. Among the antique coins the largest number — over 800 — belonged to the Thracian ruler Seuthes III, who is known as the leader of the
Thracians in their war of liberation against Alexander III and Lysimachus.
Systematic archaeological studies and the numismatic material made it possible to establish the chronology of the life of this ancient settlement. In
the time of Philip II a small Thracian settlement existed here, probably
situated around a fortified residence (tyrsis —τύρσις). Coins of Philip II
and part of the Thracian pottery belong to this settlement. A thin burnt

layer separated the ruins of this period from the upper cultural stratum, which evidenced that in the period of Seuthes III a fortified centre with the aspect of a city was built here, to which the fortifications, the stone foundations of spacious buildings, streets and various articles of Greek and Thracian origin, the coins of Seuthes III, Alexander of Macedon and the Diadochi are all to be attributed. This fortified centre was taken by storm after a siege, destroyed and plundered. The burnt sun-dried bricks and the numerous stone balls are eloquent of the tragic end of the city of Seuthes. The third period of its history, which lasted a very short time, and of which only a few insignificant restorations are left, begins with an attempt to restore the ruined city. After an interval of about 1,400 years a small mediaeval Bulgarian settlement appeared here whose inhabitants lived in flimsy buildings. The mediaeval pottery, various tools and jewellery, a poor necropolis situated in the Eastern part of the antique settlement and on Tumulus No. 1, and a large number, over 700, of mediaeval Bulgarian and Byzantine coins belong to this settlement.

Up to 1953 the name of the ancient city remained unknown. Only in October of that year, in one of the rooms of the large building — the Palace-Temple — was the first epigraphic monument of this settlement found. It proved to be at the same time the first official document to be found in Bulgaria issuing from the chancery of the Thracian rulers. The inscription is a marble slab with a pediment, 63 cm high and containing 37 lines of the Greek text of a sworn treaty between eminent personages of the ruling caste. In this case, the several last lines of the inscription are of special importance for us. They mention the existence of four copies of this inscription, two of which had been placed in Kabyle (Καβύλη) and two in Seuthopolis Σευθόπολις. The town of Kabyle is known to us from ancient literature. Its ruins are being sought for in the vicinity of the present-day town of Yambol in southern Bulgaria. The other city mentioned in the inscription is Seuthopolis, undoubtedly the newly-discovered city in which one of the copies of this inscription was found. It was thus established that the second and richest antique stratum of the newly discovered Thracian settlement was formed by the ruins of the Thracian city of Seuthopolis, unknown so far. This part of the inscription is also of very great importance because for the first time data are given in it about certain buildings in both cities, data which radically change out ideas about the Thracian city in the Early Hellenistic epoch. Kabyle is mentioned as a city with an agora, a Temple of Artemis Hecate and an Altar to Apollo. In Seuthopolis mention is also made of a Sanctuary of the Great Gods (Θεοὶ Μεγάλοι) and an altar to Dionysus, situated in the agora. These data concerning Seuthopolis given in the inscription were confirmed by the architecture and planning of the city established during the digging.

Town Plan. Seuthopolis was in dimensions a small city.[17] It consisted of a fortified settlement including an area of about 5.00 hectares, outside which, however, probably on the North side, several settlements existed, as can be judged by the roof-tiles discovered there. The form of the fortified city is outlined by the wall of the fortress, which forms a pentagon (Figs. 3, 4 and 5). Two of its sides — the south-western and the north-western — intersect at right angles. The fortified part of the town was built to a previously made plan, in conformity with the so-called regulated planning in use in the planning of the Greek polis, as early as the fifth century B.C. The architect Hippodamus of Miletus, whose name was given to this system, is considered its creator. Regular planning was particularly widespread in the Hellenistic epoch, in the time of Alexander and his successors, when the mass construction of new cities and the reconstruction of old ones was put in hand. It became characteristic of most Early Hellenistic cities in Greece, Asia Minor and Egypt. Two gates stood in the north-western and south-western walls of Seuthopolis, the only two gates of the city. Two streets, each 6 m wide, led from them to the centre of the town and delimited a large almost square place (46 x 48 m) on the west, covering an area of 2208 sq m. This was the agora of the city mentioned in the large inscription from Seuthopolis. The level of the agora is 30 cm lower than that of the surrounding streets. It was clearly delimited from them by stone borders, traces of which were found at several places. The agora took up about 1/25th of the area of the fortified city and included about 2 insulae. It was open to the principal thoroughfares on the north-east and the south-east, while various buildings were situated on the south-west and the north-west. The agora was an essential element in the structure of the city plan. In Seuthopolis it had, above all, political and religious functions. The square was empty, there was only a large altar to Dionysus on it, near which the large stone base and granite block with the inscription were found, mentioning the name of one of the priests of Dionysus, Amaistas, son of Medistas (Fig. 6). The ruins of a large building discovered along the north-western side of the agora were also probably those of a cult building.

The orthogonal plan of Greek urbanism was strictly applied in Seuthopolis in the network of streets intersecting at right angles. The orientation of the longitudinal arteries shows a deviation of -35° to the west, which was imposed by the peculiarities of the peninsula's terrain — the line of the bank, communication with the Hinterland, as well as by certain climatic considerations, such as the prevailing winds, etc. With the exception of the principal thoroughfares which are 6 m wide, the remaining streets are narrower, up to 4-3.50m. They are all paved with river cobblestones, like the agora.

A district with an area of 4620 sq m., divided from the other parts of the city by a fortified wall, was discovered in the Northern corner of the city. It has the form of a rectangle with two right angles and access to the city through a propylon on the south-eastern wall. Only one building rose on the interior, but it was the largest of all those discovered in the town. It was situated at the end, near the north-western fortress wall, symmetrically placed to the axis of the entrance. The whole space between the entrance and the building was paved with cobbles. A special feature of the plan of Seuthopolis is the close dependence between the built-up area and the fortress walls, which distinguishes it from the Greek cities. In many of them the line of the walls has no connection with the principal lines of the plan, the built-up area being frequently smaller than the space surrounded by the wall and the gates not always having a link with the principal thoroughfares.[18] In Seuthopolis, on the contrary, both the principal axes lead to the gates of the town, which is also characteristic of certain cities in Italy, which preserved the Etruscan tradition. Like most of the Greek cities, however, the buildings in Seuthopolis did not touch the fortress wall, but were separated from it by a ring-road.

Fortifications. The fortified town wall had a total length of 890 m. It was everywhere 2 m thick, with the exception of the south-eastern wall which rose directly on the bank of the Toundja. There the thickness was 1.80 m. The pentagonal form of the fort was conditioned by the configuration of the terrain. With the exception of the north-western wall, turned towards the plain, all the others followed the direction of the steep bank. Here the Toundja and its tributary formed a natural moat. On the north-western front facing the plain there were no natural obstacles. Here no artificial moat was found. However, on the other hand, the fortress wall was strengthened here by defensive installations. The north-western gate was placed exactly in the centre of this front, and was built in the form of a square tower with two passages to the plain and to the city. Square towers also probably rose at each corner of the fort. The foundations of the western, northern and north-eastern towers were very well preserved (Figs. 7, 8). Barely perceptible traces had remained of the southern corner tower, and only the tower at the eastern corner was not discovered. On the north-western front of the city the defence had been reinforced by two intermediary square towers situated at almost equal distances from the gate and the corner towers (Figs. 9, 10). The south-western front of the wall, which followed the bank at a certain distance, was reinforced instead by towers, and by bastions in the form of rectangular two-meter extensions on the outer side of the curtain (Fig. 11). Two of these bastions directly flanked the opening of the south-western gate, while the third was situated between the gate and the western corner tower (Figs. 12, 13, 14). On the remaining fronts of the fort, which are directly on the bank of the Toundja and its tributary there are no intermediary towers and bastions. It is obvious that the whole system of defence was adapted to the stronger or weaker natural protection of the place.

The situation of the inner fort, the citadel, was more special. It was originally connected with the general plan of the city, availing itself of part of the north-western and the whole north-eastern wall which defend it on the outside. Its south-western and south-eastern walls, however, were inside the city. A very large tower, defending the propylon (the entrance) was built at the southern corner. There was also an intermediary tower on its south-western wall. This fortified district occupied the north-eastern corner of the city which was also the highest point from the square of the city, although there was only a difference of 1.50 m between it and the lowest part of the city around the River Toundja. The purpose of the citadel was, above all, the defence of the palace. There was probably a fortified palace (τύρσις) here before the city was built, which was destroyed and then restored, and included in the general plan of the newly-created town.[19]

The walls and towers were built of sun-dried bricks and wood on low stone foundations. The preserved parts of them had a smooth and equal surface. The front and back faces of the foundations were made of two rows each of larger ashlars with an even outer surface. The lower course projected slightly, forming a offset on the wall. The ashlars were usually irregular in form. They were only hewn into square blocks at some places. The space between the facing was filled in with hewn stones of variou sizes, bound with mud. The sun-dried brick walls rose up on the stone foundations, levelled with wooden beams nailed together with long iron nails, considerable quantities of which were found along the whole length of the walls. Stairs led out to the breastworks of the walls and some of the towers. The place of two staircases is very clearly apparent in the stone extensions on the inside beside the western and northern corner towers. Sun-dried bricks were widely used as building material in the construction of fortified walls by the Greeks. We have a number of archaeological and written data on walls of sun-dried bricks from the sixth to the second century B.C. in Greece. In the diggings at Olynthus traces of sun-dried bricks were found on the stone plinth of fortified city walls of about the year 400. Xenophon tells of the taking of Mantinea in 385, by diverting the River Ophis towards the walls, which, since they were made of sun-dried bricks, were easily undermined and brought down. Xenophon has an interesting description of the fortified villa of Azidatus in Mysia in Asia Minor not far from Pergamum at the end of the fifth century B.C. The fortress wall of the villa was eight sun-dried bricks wide. In such a case it is possible to see in the building technique of sun-dried bricks on a stone plinth in Seuthopolis the influence of the Greek art of building, as well as the reflection of older building traditions which had struck deep roots in the peripheral regions of the Aegean world.

Dwellings and Other Buildings. The excavation at Seuthopolis gives a good idea of town dwellings in Thrace in the Early Hellenistic age.

The residential districts in Seuthopolis were distinguished by their small area which corresponded to the small dimensions of the city. In the plan of the town, as in those of the other Hellenistic cities with an orthogonal system, the insulae were the basic element, the module to which the dwellings and public squares conformed. The districts of Seuthopolis were rectangular in form with lengthened proportions, the large side along the longitudinal axes. The exact dimensions of all the insulae cannot be established, but those measuring 45 x 18 m or 150 x 60 feet predominated, according to the Attic-Euboean or Ionian system in which one foot was equal to 0.295-0.296 m. The proportion of the insulae in Seuthopolis, 5:2, are the same as the proportions of the insulae in Olynthus which, however, are twice as large in dimensions — 300 x 120 feet. The area of the agora in Seuthopolis covers two insulae, like the southern part of the square in Priene, while the citadel was built within the limits of four insulae. The two principal streets were 20 feet wide, while the width of the remaining streets was from 12 to 14 feet, which brought them close to the streets of Priene and Miletus.

The number of dwellings in one insula was not strictly established but it is possible to conclude from the better preserved foundations of dwellings in Seuthopolis that two were included in every insula. The dwellings are distinguished by their spaciousness. They include an area of between 300 and 350 sq m together with the courtyard, which formed the average area of the built-up sectors in the cities of the beginning and middle of the Hellenistic age. They are placed in such a way that they stand on two, and some even on three streets. The houses are in most cases oblong in form. The narrow south-eastern side, which is the back, lies on the transversal streets. The broad facade is turned to the longitudinal streets with the exception of Houses 1 and 5. The houses are deeper than they are wide. The proportion of width to length in these houses (Nos. 1 and 5) is 3:4 as in the houses in Priene and in Vari. In the palace and building No. 10 the proportion is 1:2. The dwellings in Seuthopolis show various types of late classical and Hellenistic Greek houses. They consist of many rooms situated around a central courtyard. The principal living rooms are on the north-western side of the courtyard, backing on the north winds coming from the Balkan Range and wide open on the south-eastern side facing the courtyard which was the source of light and heat. The dwellings show great variety in the details of their plans, a variety conditioned by the situation of the house in the insula and the placing of the entrance, which changed the position of the oikos and the andron. In most houses a large part of the foundations had, indeed, disappeared, particularly in the Eastern part of the city where the necropolis of the mediaeval settlement was. This made it impossible to reconstruct the plan of every house. In many places the presence of a house was only established by the remains of tiles or by the wells. Fortunately, however, house no. 5, whose foundations were very well preserved, enabled us fully to discover the clearly formed plan of a pastas type of dwelling (Figs. 15, 16, 17). It was placed between two parallel streets in a north-western and south-eastern direction, lying east of the principal longitudinal axis. The entrance was on the south-western side and led from the street to the inner courtyard. A covered portico — pastas, 2.60 m deep and open to the courtyard through five wooden columns standing on square stone bases, preserved in situ, ran along its north-western side. Two large rooms were entered through the portico. The first was used as a storeroom for foodstuffs, while in the second a hearth-altar was found in the middle. This part of the house included the oikos, the living rooms with the kitchen in the northern corner of the house. On the north-east, on the same axis as the entrance, lay the andron (the reception room) with a columned porch or ante-room. The foundations of a staircase leading to the second floor were discovered along its western wall. It was restricted only to above the north and the north-west wing of the house, a gallery lying above the pastas. In house no. 5 there was also a small room for the slave-porter, situated on the south side of the entrance. We are familiar with a classical example of a pastas type of house from the Hellenistic dwellings in Olynthus dating back to the end of the classical epoch.[20] This type is to be found in different variants. The portico could be placed on all sides of the courtyard, when it became a peristyle. The intermediary variants are the examples with two or three porticoes, but one of them is always longer and broader and remains a pastas. The houses of the peristyle type with Northern portico-pastas are widespread besides in Olynthus in a number of regions of Continental and Island Greece, Asia Minor and the colonies at the end of the classical and particularly during the Hellenistic epoch. House no. 1 in Seuthopolis very much recalls the peristyle type of dwelling in plan (Fig. 18). Rooms on all sides surround a central rectangular courtyard, being in two rows on the south-western side. The entrance was probably on the north-eastern side. Their type cannot be clearly grasped in the plans of the other houses. Other forms appear there, of which, because these dwellings were not well preserved and also because

11

we are not familiar with the Thracian dwelling, we cannot say in how far they continued a local tradition and in how far they were influenced by Greek architecture (Figs. 19, 20, 21).

House no. 10, 23.50 m long and 10 m wide, has a most interesting plan (Figs. 22, 23). Three of its sides give on streets — to the north-east on the principal longitudinal street, which runs from the north-western city gate, to the north-west on a street at right angles to the principal street, while on the south-east it comes out on the agora. It consists of ten rectangular rooms, placed in two rows, forming five double rooms connected by entrances between them. Their dimensions are almost the same, with the exception of the middle pair which is smaller. This is where the main entrance to the building was on the north-eastern side from the principal street. The courtyard probably lay on the south-western side. The three stone bases of the wooden colonnade can be linked with it. The curious plan of the building — a long and narrow one, following the principal street along its longitudinal axis, as well as the finds and coins which came to light in its rooms, give grounds for it to be considered as a building connected with commercial activities.

The dwellings in Seuthopolis were built on foundations of hewn stones bound with mud. The superstructure was of lath and plaster, a wooden skeleton filled with sun-dried bricks. The roofing consisted of a wooden grill covered with boards and plastered with clay on which broad flat tiles were arranged, tegulae (solenes) of the Corinthian form familiar in Greek architecture. The gaps between them were covered with semi-cylindrical curved tiles, imbrices (kalypteres) of the Laconian type. In general, in the plan of city and dwellings, as well as in the building technique Seuthopolis showed close links with the Hellenistic building traditions which, however, took Thracian life into consideration. A characteristic feature of the Seuthopolis house was the presence of small clay hearth-platforms of a square shape on the floor of one of the principal rooms (Fig. 24). They were richly ornamented by having various ornaments stamped on the damp plaster with a cord: concentric circles and rectangles, garlands of ivy leaves and twigs, rosettes, etc. The surface of one such platform had been coloured red and blue. All this goes to show that these little platforms were not simple hearths, but were ἐσχάραι , domestic hearth-altars, connected with the cult (see Chapter IV).

The most considerable building in Seuthopolis was the one in the fortified district (the citadel); it was placed at right angles to the axis of the propylon, at the monumental entrance of which the foundations of a stone plinth have been preserved (Figs. 25, 26). The parts of the only column found in the city — a Doric capital and the lowest drum with a square base — may have come from the propylon (Fig. 27). The echinus of the capital has an almost rectilinear contour which fully corresponds to the time, the turn of the fourth and third century, when the Doric capital lost the elasticity of its profile. The drum was cut from a block together with the broad pediment, which was unusual for Doric columns and ancient Greek architecture. It is obvious that this violation of the canon was permitted by the men who made it — Thracian stonemasons and master builders — under the influence of local conditions and demands.

The large building was erected at the end of a large courtyard (temenos), quadrangular in form and including an area of about 0.4 ha, paved with river stones. The building itself has an extremely interesting and original plan (Figs. 28, 29). An ante-chamber, 40 m wide and about 5 m deep, situated along the length of the building, leads to its interior. Its facade probably had a colonnade. The interior of the building is most irregularly divided. Almost the whole eastern half is separated into a spacious hall, 18 m long and 12 m wide (Fig. 30). Its entrance is on the side of the ante-chamber. The remaining half of the building is divided into three double rooms, isolated from one another, but each pair communicating with each other and with the common ante-chamber (Figs. 31, 32). A staircase, leading to the second floor, was found in the inner section of the middle room. The building material is the same as in the remaining buildings in Seuthopolis. Because they had been severely burnt the sun-dried bricks of which the walls above the stone plinth had been built, were well-preserved here. The imbrices along the edge of the roof ended in antefixes ornamented with palmettes (Fig. 33). This was undoubtedly the most monumental building in Seuthopolis, and its inner brilliance certainly did not yield pride of place to its exterior. Remains of rich plastering were found in the great hall. Stucco work had been placed on a four-layer foundation, and imitates marble incrustation; there was a band of black orthostats below, above it a broad projecting strip imitating multi-coloured marble, and the remaining part of the walls in the hall were covered with Pompeian red. In its spaciousness and decoration this hall was a real red ceremonial reception room in which the black band of orthostats formed a contrast with the white marble imitation of the ceiling. This type of stuccowork, imitating the so-called incrustation decoration of the rich buildings in ancient Greece, is known to us in Bulgaria from the system of decoration of the celebrated Kazanluk tomb, which lies 7-8 km east of Seuthopolis.[21] This manner of decoration is also well known from the decoration of the houses in Olynthus, Delos, Priene, etc.[22] It is of interest that in this room, where Hellenistic decoration reigns supreme, a hearth-altar is also to be found which is not characteristic of the contemporary Greek buildings. A hearth-altar like this one was also found in one of the other rooms near which the Great Inscription was found. The special plan of the building, its decoration and its situation in the plan of the city in a separate, strongly fortified district, leaves no doubt that this was the personal residence-palace of Seuthes III. The circumstance that it was precisely in this building that one of the slabs with the inscription was found, and that we established the place of the altar of Dionysus in the agora, where the second slab should have been found, makes us accept, according to the data of the inscription, that the residence of Seuthes III fulfilled several functions. Along with the large throne-room and ceremonial hall in the eastern part of the building and the living rooms on the west, the Sanctuary of the Great Gods of Samothrace had been included in the double room next to the reception room. This architectural uniting of Sanctuary and Palace of the Thracian ruler corresponds to the double functions which the King had — religious and political power were united in his person. It is, however, possible that the priestly functions of the ruler were limited to the most important cult only, in this case the cult of the Cabeiroi.

The composition of the whole architectural ensemble of the fortified district, the citadel with its propylon and the axial situation of the palace, recall in the most general features the Beuleuterion and the Gymnasium in Miletus.[23]   The plan of the palace-temple, however, finds its closest parallels in the plan of the Herakleion (the Sanctuary of Herakles) on the Island of Thasos.[24] It had undergone a radical reconstruction at the end of the fourth century when it was formed of five rooms with an entrance giving onto the ante-chamber, 5 m wide and 36 m long. Of course, there is a considerable difference in the inner distribution: there is no large hall in the Herakleion, the rooms are single, on one axis. However, this corresponds to the features and the special purpose of the two buildings.

The diggings showed that Seuthopolis was not only a correctly planned city, as were the Hellenistic cities built from the fifth century onward; like them it had sewerage in the houses and in the city. Drains, consisting of clay pipes or of other curved tiles covering one another, were discovered in many dwellings. They all led to common drains which were situated in the middle of the streets, and chiefly along those which ran from the north-west to the south-east with a slope towards the south-eastern fortress wall. Here, at various places in the fortress wall there were openings with out-falls, through which rain and the waste water of the city were poured into the River Toundja.

Water was supplied to the city only by wells. A well, built of stones, in the form of a cylinder or a prism, was found in the courtyard of every dwelling. One of the wells was built of bricks (Fig. 34).

The scale of construction in Seuthopolis which required large funds, indicates the great economic possibilities of Seuthes III and his heightened political importance. The city was built according to a previously conceived plan, realized in a short time as a complex ensemble, by order of the King, just as we have a number of examples in the urbanising activity of Alexander III and his successors. Seuthes did not stand aside from the fashions of his time and in building his capital he adopted the principles of the ancient art of town building, as well as the example of the other Hellenistic rulers, in giving it his own name. The city was built after Seuthes' successful clashes with the Macedonians, probably at the beginning of the last quarter of the fourth century B.C.

CHAPTER II

ECONOMIC LIFE

1. AGRICULTURE

The numerous archaeological finds which came to light in Seuthopolis revealed many sides of the culture of its inhabitants and the economy of the town in the Early Hellenistic age.

Farming and stockbreeding were important branches of agriculture. No remains of cereals were found, but traces of straw are clearly to be seen in the pieces of plaster from the walls of the dwellings, since it was mixed with the clay to give resilience to the mixture. Besides this, large numbers of pithoi, clay jars, were found in the town, which were used to store cereals. Wheat was ground in primitive querns, but better made millstones known from Olynthus, Delos, Priene and the towns along the Northern Black Sea coast were found in many houses (Fig. 35). Several iron ploughshares with a small spoon-shaped lower part and a long flat handle narrowing towards the top, where it curved like a hook, perpendicularly outward, were also found at the Seuthopolis dig (Fig. 36). Although it is still difficult to say with certainty to what kind of plough a ploughshare of this kind was attached, the use of a plough with iron parts is proof of the high technology used by the Thracians in cultivating the land.[25]

Conditions around Seuthopolis were favourable for the development of viticulture. During digging several curved knives made of iron were found (pruning knives) with which the vine stocks were pruned.

The tremendous amount of bones of domestic animals show that stockbreeding was highly developed.[26] The bones of cattle, cows and oxen predominate among them, but the abundance of other bones shows the great extent to which sheep, goats and pigs were bred. The bones of horses are found in comparatively smaller quantities. Numerous finds of weights for looms and spindles, which came to light in almost every house, showed the extensive development of home spinning and weaving, which was closely connected with the development of stockbreeding.

The proximity of the swiftly-flowing Tonsos and its tributaries made fishing an important means of livelihood for the population. Considerable quantities of weights for fishing nets, made of tiles or the bottoms of clay vessels, shaped like discs with a hole in the middle, were found in almost every house. Hunting was one of the favourite pastimes of the Thracians. The large quantity of bones from boars, bears, stags and deer found in Seuthopolis indicates that there were large tracts of forests full of game in the surroundings of the city and in the nearby mountains. These bones are an important source for the study of the fauna in the Thracian lands in antiquity. An important find in this respect is that of the skull and horns of an aurochs (Urus bos primigenius).

The skilled Thracian craftsmen used the horns of animals, chiefly of stags, to make handles for knives and other articles. Many pieces of cut and polished stag horns for the making of handles were found in one of the rooms of House No 1.

2. MANUFACTURE AND MINOR ARTS

Pottery. The local vessels, found in abundance in Seuthopolis, are evidence of the extensive production of pottery. In technique it can be divided into two groups: hand-made pottery, and pottery thrown on a wheel.

Thracian hand-made pottery forms an original group of the local pottery which was used by the masses of the population. It includes various vessels for everyday needs, and also others used in the cult and the ritual of burial. There does not seem to have been any strict differentiation in the use of these vessels. Forms of vessels characteristic of those used in daily life are also found in the cemeteries. A characteristic feature of this group of pottery is that it is more roughly made of clay containing a considerable quantity of sand, quartz or mica, which gave greater resilience to the clay, and made the eva- poration of water in drying the vessels quicker. In one class of vessels the clay has smaller admixtures, the form is more regular, the walls were equally thick and well-smoothed. It is possible that a primitive wheel was used in giving them their final shape. The ornamentation of the rough vessels was added before they were baked. It consisted of bands in relief, made separately and carefully stuck onto the walls with diluted clay. Most of the bands were broken by hollows, little pits or slanting incisions made with the aid of a point or by the pressure of a finger. Various other elements were added on to the bands or the walls of the vessels, protuberances in the form of tongues or buds, spirals in relief, swastikas, etc. Some of them, such as arc-shaped adfixes, served as handles. Perpendicular handles with oval or rectangular cross- sections were also added on after the pot was made. The walls of the vessels were smoothed in different ways. After the rougher vessels had dried they were smoothed with a wet rag or a tuft of grass, which is clearly apparent from the traces left on the surface. In other vessels the surface was slightly polished, for which wooden or bone smoothers 3-4 mm wide were used. The hand-working of the rough vessels gives grounds for the supposition that producing them was part of the functions of the domestic economy and was usually done by women. However, the presence of a certain standardization of the forms, despite the conservative and primitive technology, proves on the other hand that the pro- duction of some of these vessels was the work of craftsmen in workshops, where the professional level of the work was high.

There is not much variety of form in this group of vessels. The most characteristic of them are large vessels of a cylindrical or bell shape, 20 to 40 cm high (Figs 37, 38). They are found in all the archaeological centres in Thrace from the fifth to the third century B.C.[27] The finds from Seutho- polis show their extensive use in daily life: for storing foodstuffs and for cooking. At the same time they were used as funerary urns in a number of Thracian mound burials of the fourth to third century B.C. The older tradi- tions of pottery in the Bronze and Early Iron Age undoubtedly influenced the development of this form. Close parallels to this group of Thracian vessels are to be found in the settlements and cemeteries of Romania and the forest-steppe regions of Moldavia up to the Dniester, where a tribal ethnocultural centre in which the predominant ethnic element was Northern Thracian was apparent.

Another basic form of Thracian pottery made by hand was a deep dish in the form of a truncated cone with four arc-shaped handles placed cross-wise under the edge of the mouth.

Cups which, in numbers, come second after the cylindrical vessels, had a considerable share in the hand-made pottery. They formed two sub-groups: those with handles and those without.

Cups with a perpendicular handle were cylindrical in form, had an even bottom and were ornamented with bands in relief broken up by small pits and tongue-like protuberances. They varied in height between 10 and 19 cm. Smaller cups (5 to 11 cm high) were found together with them; they were ornamented below the mouth with a row of small cone-like buds. Similar cups have been found in Thracian centres in North and South Bulgaria. Almost no local features were found in the pottery forms from different regions, which is a sign of an increased trend towards the material and cultural unity of Thrace in this period.

A characteristic feature of the second group of cups was the lack of a handle. They were small in size, were shaped like truncated cones or cylinders, with an even bottom and a straight ridge around the mouth, under which there was a design of buds in relief.

The last group included a number of small vessels cylindrical in form or pear- or egg-shaped, from 5 to 10 cm high, which were pots for melting small quantities of metal.

Three roughly-worked lamps of curious local forms were also found (Fig. 39). One of them repeated the form of the lamps of the Hellenistic age with a round flat reservoir and a protruding wick-holder.

The hand-worked pottery is an important component of Thracian culture, and a valuable source for the study of the way of life of the population of Seuthopolis. Although made by hand, in most cases the vessels are well proportioned in form, are carefully worked and ornamented in various ways. The thrown pottery, imported or locally made, had practically no influence on its development and shows the stability of the original traditions of Thracian pottery. The finding of this rough pottery in Seuthopolis in almost the same quantity as the thrown pottery in the houses of the rich Thracians definitely shows that it was not used by the poor population alone. Alongside the wheel-made Thracian pottery and the imported Greek pottery the hand-made pottery had its own independent place and was widely used for definite needs in life and in cult.

Thracian wheel-made pottery includes the entire variety of vessels used in everyday life and in cult. The vessels were most skilfully made of well-purified and worked clay which, after baking, acquired a grey or red colour. The difference in the colour was due to the way in which the grey pottery was baked, as it was done under special conditions, with a restricted access of oxygen; however, regardless of the colour, the forms of the vessels are identical. The early introduction of the potter's wheel into Thrace about the middle of the sixth century B.C. gave a strong impetus to the development of pottery, which already had the character of a craft in Seuthopolis. Work on the wheel allowed the Thracian potter to attain a great variety of forms and details in his vessels. A smooth and harmonious form is characteristic of his work, with pure lines and a smooth curve of the outlines. Ornamentation is modest, usually consisting of horizontally incised or impressed lines which emphasized the individual parts of the vessel. Polished, wavy bands are also found. A stamped decoration of rosettes was found on one jug. A slip, a solution of diluted clay poured over the surface, was a characteristic feature of the Thracian vessels. After this was done these vessels, particularly the grey ones, were given a high polish, resulting in an almost metallic brilliance of a silvery-grey or lead-grey surface. On several fragments decoration consisted of bands in relief with slanting incisions, which indicates the influence of the rough pottery.

Many fragments of broad-bottomed grey amphorae, with short cylindrical necks and two handles, repeating a well-known classical Greek form, were found in Seuthopolis. Deep vessels with a krater shape, their rim curving outward around the mouth, were also extensively used (Fig. 40). Below the mouth two arc-shaped handles were stuck to the walls. Vessels of this form were used as urns in many Thracian burials of the fifth to fourth century B.C. Vessels for fluids — jugs, ewers, oinochoe and kantharos-like cups — were particularly widespread.[28] About 50 well-preserved ewers and oinochoi with rounded or egg-shaped bodies, high slender necks and rims slightly curving outward were found in Seuthopolis (Figs 41, 42). The handles were perpendicular, raised above the mouth and ending in the upper half of the body. These vessels are between 11 and 20 cm high. All the vessels of this group have harmonious lines, correct proportions and are well made. Close parallels to them are to be found in a number of Thracian tumuli and sites from the turn of the fourth and third century B.C.

Fragments of better preserved types of cups of the kantharos form with rounded or double-cone-shaped bodies were also found. The lower part is smooth or ornamented with incised perpendicular lines which imitate the grooves of the Greek kantharoi (Fig. 43).

Deep dishes in the form of a truncated cone turned upside down are another type of vessel frequently found in Seuthopolis (Fig. 44). They have a slightly thickened and inward curving rim around the mouth, the bottom is placed on a low ring-like stand. This was a form well-known in Thrace in the Bronze and the Early Iron Age, but it had undoubtedly undergone the influence of the Greek bowls of the fifth to fourth century.

Fish plates, which were imitations of the Greek black-glaze fish dishes, were also widely used in Seuthopolis. The Thracian dishes were made of grey or red clay and had thicker walls (Fig. 45).

Fragments of askoi, lekythoi and lacrimaria, local imitations of Greek forms, were also found. One deep cup with a semi-spherical body and a high neck with concave walls, having an omphalos on the rounded bottom, was of great interest. It was made of red clay and covered with a slip. The graceful form and its pure line show the strong influence of silver bowls (Fig. 46).

A rare vessel, a _kernos_, was also found in Seuthopolis (Fig. 47). It is a hollow ring with a diameter of 23 cm, made of red clay with four small cups (_kotiliskoi_) attached to it, which are identical in form with the cup described above. The existence of the _kernos_ has been recorded in Crete, in the early period of the Creto-Mycenaean culture. The fourth century B.C. finds in Eleusis are most important in establishing the changes in its form and use in Greece as a ritual vessel in the cult of Eleusis.

Several grey clay lamps were found, based on familiar antique types. One has three wicks and was thrown. It had a deep round reservoir, a flat disc with a large opening and three protruding wick-holders. The remaining two lamps were made with the aid of a mould and were shaped like negroes' heads, with flat noses, low foreheads and curly hair. The protruding and open mouth serves as the opening of the wick-holder. The oil was poured into the lamp through a large opening at the back of the head (Fig. 48).

The forms of thrown pottery examined above clearly show that most of them were closely connected with ancient Greek pottery. A number of Thracian vessels repeated the forms created in the Early Hellenistic age, while some had parallels in far older vessels of the classical, and even of the archaic and Creto-Mycenaean epochs. The Thracian potter carefully imitated the Greek forms, but he often further developed and changed the prototypes, depending on local taste and needs.

Pithoi and Stamps on the Mouths of Pithoi. An important place in the output of pottery in Seuthopolis was held by _pithoi_, used to store various foods: cereals, wine, dried fish, etc. They were therefore closely linked with agriculture, hence the extent of their production. Several hundred fragments of mouths, walls and bases and about 15 whole, well preserved _pithoi_ were found scattered all over Seuthopolis (Fig. 49). Several _pithoi_ were also discovered in the earth of Mound No 3, which belongs to the necropolis of Seuthopolis. The form of these _pithoi_, as can be concluded from the samples preserved, did not differ essentially from that of this type of vessel discovered elsewhere. An egg-shaped body with a wide mouth and short neck narrows down to the pointed bottom which ends in a short cylindrical foot. The rim around the mouth is thick and shaped in a variety of profiles. There are different sizes of _pithoi_: from 0.95 m height and 0.71 m at the widest part of the body, to 1.45 m in height and 1.05 m in width. The clay, usually mixed with grains of quartz, had acquired a brick red colour in baking.

The stamps, 143 in number, and placed on the mouth of the vessels, are of particular interest in the _pithoi_ of Seuthopolis.[29] Their study poses many problems, all the more so in that a very restricted number of stamps on _pithoi_ were known before.

The newly discovered material from Seuthopolis is actually the only and the largest collection of stamps on _pithoi_, the study of which is very greatly facilitated by the fact that they were found in a centre whose existence can be placed within a comparatively narrow chronological framework, determined with certainty — from the middle of the fourth to the middle of the third century B.C.

The stamps of Seuthopolis can be divided into two main groups. All the stamps placed on the mouths of the vessels before they were baked belong to the first group, which is considerably more numerous. The second group includes signs incised on the mouths after the vessels were baked.

The stamps of the first group, which are distinguished by their great variety, contain incised or stamped letters, signs and emblems (Figs 50, 51).

On nine fragments of mouths the stamps are composed of various letters. The letter Σ is met with three times, and in all three cases it has been stamped on. In two fragments from one and the same vessel the die used was round with a diameter of 2 cm, and in the third it was rectangular, 2.6 x 1.6 cm.

On four fragments the letter K is found, carefully written with deeply incised lines. The profiles of all four fragments are the same: in two parts with a projecting edge in the middle. The clay is also the same. The letter $\curlyvee$, 6 and 7 cm high, is incised on the two other fragments.

The most frequently met symbol is one like an arrow ($\curlyvee$), placed on 18 fragments with its tip pointing to the inner rim of the mouth. All symbols are deeply incised with the perpendicular line from 3 to 6 cm long. Three types of profiles can be differentiated in this group.

The sign W is found on 6 fragments, from 2.5 to 3.5 cm high. The profile of all fragments in this group is the same: a projecting edge in relief in the middle.

The remaining stamps are emblems distinguished by the great variety in the emblems depicted.

The round stamps, which are the most numerous, are made with round dies. Among them are the dies which are a circle, 2 cm in diameter, without a frame, with a cross in relief inscribed in it. On an almost complete mouth six stamps of this kind have been preserved, while there are four on another one.

The group of stamps depicting rosettes is extremely varied.

On five fragments there is a deeply stamped eight-leaf rosette with a diameter of 4.5 cm. Three rosettes, situated at 120° from one another, are stamped on a whole mouth.

A five-leaf rosette, diameter 2.5 cm, was found on three fragments, and on two fragments, probably from one and the same vessel, a six-leaf rosette (diameter 5.5 cm) had been stamped.

One stamp, depicting an eight-leaf rosette (diameter 2 cm), with narrow pointed leaves shows very fine workmanship.

Rectangular Stamps. All marks of this group were also stamped. On four fragments the stamp was a rectangular space, 3.5 x 3 cm, in which two semi-circles, their arcs turned to the centre of the space, were depicted. These emblems strongly recall the decoration of the Aegean altars.

Another rectangular stamp, 3.6 x 2.6 cm, had two diagonally crossing lines, thickened at their ends, which, taking an amphora stamp from Thasos as analogous, can be explained as torches.

A third large group of stamps depicts jewellery. [30] On eight fragments there are concave images of pendants from earrings, which show open rings with cone-shaped thickened ends turned outward. A certain number of the same type of earring pendants have been found in Thrace, in the rich burials of the necropolis at Douvanliy. Pendants of this type were also worn in Seuthopolis, where we found two of them.

On four fragments the stamps show fibulae, three of which are of the Thracian type, while the fourth is snake-like.

One stamp shows a piece of jewellery, probably a metal plaque. Four stamps were made with the help of intaglios. There is a very clear imprint of an intaglio depicting an exquisite scene — a lion attacking a horse.

Another group of stamps on five fragments depicted an ornamental motif of spirals, combined in various ways, a design widespread in ancient art.

Of cult articles the double axe was shown, while two stamps could be interpreted as the schematic image of a human figure.

A proportion of the stamps on pithoi from Seuthopolis, consisting of monograms and individual letters imprinted with the aid of special stamps, are undoubtedly abbreviations of names, which should be connected with the owners of pottery workshops. The stamp with the letter Σ deserves special attention, as it could be the initial letter of the king's name Σεύθης , representing the mark stamped on the output of the royal potteries, i.e. of the state pottery workshops.

Another group of stamps are signs deeply imprinted before the vessels were baked, and were also used as a distinctive mark, certifying that the pithoi belonged to a definite workshop.

The remaining stamps are anepigraphic and consisted only of an emblem. In contrast to the Greek stamp-emblems, which were single, there are often three stamps on the pithoi of Seuthopolis, placed at equal distances on the mouth. In only one case were there six stamps, but the mouth was not completely preserved and there may possibly have been nine stamps.

Despite the markedly ornamental character of the stamps in this group it cannot be accepted that they were decorative in function. Their principal aim and intention was to serve as emblems of the potters' workshops, i.e. of the owners of these workshops. This was a widespread custom of the ceramic industry in the Hellenistic age.

A great variety of subjects is characteristic of the Seuthopolis stamp-emblems. While in part of them the origin of the design is not clear, in others the source of influence is quite apparent. Some of the seals in Seuthopolis were obviously made under the impact of the Thasos amphora stamps, which is reflected both in the form and the images: a circle with an inscribed cross, rosettes, etc. Several rectangular stamps show a close connection with the images of cult monuments, altars, etc., of the Mycenaean epoch. Other stamps are imprints of intaglios.

Jewellery also served as models of emblems — pendents of earrings, fibulae, etc. Of these the fibulae are of special importance, being of the so-called

Thracian type widespread in the lands of the Thracians in the fifth to third
century B.C. The original pieces of jewellery were used as stamps in most
cases. The presence of the Thracian _fibula,_ a characteristic local form, as
a stamp on pithoi from Seuthopolis is sufficient proof that these vessels were
made in Thrace. The emblems, whose designs can be compared with Thracian
coins of the fifth to fourth century, support this opinion. This is the double
axe and particularly the eight-leaf rosette, which calls to mind the rosette
placed on some of the bronze coins minted by Seuthes III. The constant presence of the double axe and the eight-leaf rosette on the coins of the Odrysaean
kings and tribes give grounds for us to see in the Seuthopolis stamps the mani-
festation of a general Thracian symbolism. The use of these symbols as
marks on pottery enables us to consider them as royal seals. There may have
been royal workshops for the production of _pithoi_ and bricks in Seuthopolis, if
we accept that the letter Ϛ found on both types of ceramic articles stood for
the name of the king.

Private persons, who also began to mark their work with a definite mark,
could also have been the owners of the workshops. Each workshop had a large
number of stamps, which may explain the differences in dimensions and details of one and the same mark. Moreover, the _pithoi_ with the same marks
have small wreaths of the same dimensions and profiles, and often the same
composition of the clay, which shows the close dependence between these elements in the production of each individual workshop.

The large number of pithoi with stamps found in Seuthopolis should not
surprise us. On the one hand, regular digging was done here over an extensive area, during which almost the whole city was uncovered. On the other
hand, the principal enterprises and, above all, the potteries were situated
around Seuthopolis, as they were around all large political centres.

Graffiti. Sixteen fragments, on which numbers or individual letters were
scratched after baking, belong to the second group of stamped _pithoi_ mouths.

On 10 fragments of mouths the graffiti are numbers, expressed in letters,
in accordance with the Greek acrophonic system.[31] Four of the numbers are
of high values — H 𐊠ΔΓ (165), E ϒΔΙΙΙ (163), HϒΓ (155), and 𐊠ΔΔΙ(71). Two
signs are used for the number 100: H, as is usually found in the Attic system,
and the letter E, used in Chios, Tauric Chersonese, etc. Two signs are also
used for 50: 𐊠 used twice, as is the customary expression in the Attic system,
and the sign ϒ used in Chalcedon, Tauric Chersonese, etc. This sign is
found with the same value on a _pithos_ from Callatis and on a fragment from
North Bulgaria, on the surrounding rims of which the numerals ϒΓΙΙΙ (58) and
ϒΔΓΙΙ(67) were scratched respectively.

Since only numbers are given on the fragments from Seuthopolis considered
here, without any indication of the unit of measurement which should be understood, the figures can be interpreted in two ways. They could indicate the
capacity of the vessel or its price. In the _pithoi_ of Olynthus Robinson rejects
the possibility of the numerals indicating anything but their price. If we allow
that he is right, and accept that the price of the vessels is marked on the four
fragments from Seuthopolis, very large sums are obtained: 163, 165, 155
and 71 drachmae: sums which pithoi are hardly likely to have cost in antiquity.
All the more so as data on the value of one type of vessel have been preserved

in certain inscriptions, vessels which in dimensions and intended use were close to pithoi and which only cost 9 to 11 drachms. Moreover, in figures signifying sums, monetary signs were usually placed before or after the numeral or connected with it, and in this case they are lacking. It should not be forgotten that in the case of large vessels like the pithoi, which were chiefly used for storing various kinds of foodstuffs, it was most important to note their capacity. It is quite clear, moreover, that the figures under consideration do not indicate the price but the capacity of the vessels, as this was often marked on various vessels in antiquity. Thus, about 100 sherds of amphorae, pithoi and other vessels with numerals scratched on them were found in the Athenian Agora.[32] Of them the capacity of the vessel is marked on 61 sherds, while in only 9 cases, and not with certainty at that, is the price indicated. Unfortunately the four numerals from Seuthopolis now engaging our attention were not found on whole vessels, so that there is no possibility of measuring their capacity and determining the unit of measurement which should be understood. Nevertheless, in order to have an approximate idea of the capacity of the pithoi from Seuthopolis we have used the whole pithoi found in the city. Thus, one of the large pithoi found in House No 5, height 1.34 m, width 1.04 m, diameter of the mouth 0.59 m and of the bottom 0.15 m, contained about 530 litres, and one of the small pithoi, height 1.10 m, width 0.76 m, diameter of the mouth 0.41 m and of the bottom 0.135 m, contained 225 litres. If we accept that the pithos bearing the highest number, 165, contained 535 litres, the unit of measurement obtained by dividing the two figures is 3.24. If we divide the capacity of the smallest pithos with the smallest number indicated on the mouth, the figure 3.24 is again obtained. It actually corresponds to the Greek liquid measure κοτύλη . The same measure is usually also used in indicating the capacity of amphorae and pithoi on the vessels from the Athenian agora. We have no grounds for interpreting the numbers 165, 163, 155 and 71 in another way except as signifying the capacity of the pithoi and to understand the measure κοτύλη in the indications on the Seuthopolis vessels.

On a second group of sherds from the mouths of pithoi numerals have also been scratched, again according to the acrophonic system, but they are far smaller in value. The number ΔΔ (20) is met with once, the number ΔΙ (11) twice, the number Δ (10) once, ΓΙΙ (7) once and ΙΙΙΙ (4) once. It cannot be said with certainty whether these numerals indicate the capacity of the vessels or their value. If, however, we accept that they, too, should be linked with the vessel's capacity, in this case we should understand not κοτύλη but a larger measure — perhaps medimne.

The study of the numerals indicated on the pithoi of Seuthopolis is an important contribution to the question of the spread and use of the acrophonic system of numerals in the Early Hellenistic age in regions bordering on Greece. They also offer valuable information on the cultural history of Seuthopolis, where both the numeral and the metric Early Hellenistic systems were known and used by its inhabitants.

Bricks. The dig at Seuthopolis also brought to light a variety of bricks. The bricks used for tombs, wells, small platforms, etc., and a large number of individual bricks, scattered all over the town, make it possible to establish many details about the form, size, manner of making and use of bricks by the Thracians in the Early Hellenistic age.[33]

The bricks found at Seuthopolis are large, strong, well-baked and made of fine well-mixed clay in which quartz grains and larger pebbles are found in rare cases. When baked the clay acquired a clear red colour.

In form, the bricks fall into two groups: rectangular and trapezoid bricks. The latter show a sectoral cross-cut with two parallel, slightly curved arcs (the inner one shorter and concave, the outer one longer and convex) and two straight not parallel sides. A great variety in size is to be observed in both types of bricks (Fig. 52). The dimensions of the rectangular bricks are: from 0.54 x 0.42 x 0.068 m for the largest to 0.34 x 0.32 x 0.06 for the smallest.

The size of the trapezoid bricks also varies: from 0.45 height x 0.36 (upper arc) — 0.29 (lower arc) x 0.07 m thickness of the largest bricks to 0.385 (0.375) x 0.265 - 0.17 x 0.06 m of the smallest.

A special type of brick is met with in the rectangular and the trapezoid bricks with a short slantingly cut side, not obtained by additional lopping, but when the brick was shaped in a special mould.

The fact that all the narrow sides of the brick and one of the broad flat surfaces (which we shall conditionally call the face) have an extremely smooth surface on which strips of the structure of wood are imprinted, while the second wide side (the back) is rough, gives us grounds to assert that the bricks were made with the aid of wooden moulds which were not just rectangular frames, but also had a bottom. A piece of clay was placed in the mould and pressed well down to the bottom and the sides of the mould, so that the brick could be given the desired form. The back of the brick, which lay at the top of the mould, was probably smoothed with a wooden or metal spatula. The mould was then turned and the brick left to dry on the ground, before being baked with the right side up. That is why all the imprints of the tracks of animals and birds and the footsteps of people, who trod on the damp and unbaked bricks, are only to be found on the smooth broad face of the brick.

Fingerprints have been left on several bricks. All the fingerprints are on the end of the long unparallel sides which lie closer to the wide side at the back. Obviously the brickmaker sometimes used his hands to help get the brick out of the mould.

Stamps, lacking in variety, were found on a number of bricks. They are usually sunken rectangles or individual letters placed on the brick before it was baked. The letter T was inscribed in a rectangular area on one fragment of a square brick. The letters were placed on the broad face or back surfaces. There are five perpendicular parallel lines on one brick, on another we see the letter H, while on three bricks the letter Ϟ appears, which should be linked with the owner of the brick yard (Fig. 53). This could be the initial of the king's name, which gives grounds to see, here too, state workshops along with the workshops of private producers. The large quantity of bricks (in Seuthopolis and its necropolis more than 1000 of them were found) and their variety of forms and sizes indicate that this branch of the pottery industry in Seuthopolis at the turn of the fourth and third century B.C. had reached great prosperity and had developed as a result of the new needs of construction. What were these needs? It has been seen that the large part of the bricks found in the city itself were inidividual finds, others came from drains, wells and small platforms (furnaces or hearths) (Fig. 54). However, the great variety of bricks in format and dimensions in each of these sites, and the use in individual cases of pieces of brick as well, indubitably indicates that the brick material in the city at these sites was accidental material at hand, used secondarily after certain older buildings for which they had been intended, had been destroyed. The only place in the city where we find uniform rectangular bricks of the same dimensions, systematically arranged, was the brick paving at the cistern. Obviously the appearance of bricks in Seuthopolis was not dictated by the needs of ordinary housing construction, in whose straight-lined plan trapezoid bricks would have been quite out of place. What is more, as the digging showed, sun-dried bricks were the basic material used in building the dwellings of Seuthopolis. Their instability and the ease with which they disintegrated under the action of water is the reason for which we do not have a large number of well-preserved sun-dried bricks at our disposal. It was only at the Palace, where the fire which destroyed the building baked the mud bricks that fully preserved samples were found. They were made of clay abundantly mixed with straw which gave them greater resilience. Their dimensions were 0.50 x 0.40 by 0.09 m.

The only buildings in which bricks were used as material specially prepared for the purpose are the three beehive tombs in Tumulus 2 and Tumulus 3 in Seuthopolis and in the Kazanluk tomb discovered not far from Seuthopolis.

It is precisely the original plan and construction of the beehive tombs which can alone explain the appearance of the rich variety of forms and dimensions which we found in the bricks of Seuthopolis.

As the preserved parts of the beehive tomb in Tumulus No 3 quite clearly proves, the trapezoid bricks were intended, above all, for the building of round chambers: a plan shown by the domed chambers. However, in the dromos, whose plan is rectangular, only rectangular bricks have been used. This was confirmed by the several rectangular bricks preserved in the dromos of the destroyed beehive tomb in Tumulus No 2. The several bands of the vault of the dromos preserved in the tomb of Tumulus No 3, also show us the manner in which the vaulting of this tomb was accomplished, i.e. by the gradual corbelling of the bands of bricks going upward. In this way a triangular vault was obtained, whose walls were not smooth, but had many profiles. This type of vault is familiar to us from the tombs in South Russia where, however, instead of bricks, stone blocks had been used. The same system of vaulting was used in the round chamber in Tumulus No 2 and 3, with a beehive dome formed by gradual corbelling of the rows of bricks going upward. In this type of vault, when ordinary rectangular or trapezoid bricks with perpendicular narrow sides were used, a vault with profiled walls was obtained which could not be used for mural paintings. To avoid this inconvenience, when the tomb was to be decorated with murals rectangular and trapezoid bricks with a narrow slanted inner side were used. In such a case, the vault of the dromos and the dome of the round chamber were given a smooth surface on the inside which it was possible to cover with plaster.

It was exactly this type of trapezoid bricks with a slanting inner wall which were used in the domed round chamber in the Kazanluk tomb, well-known for its frescoes.

Establishing brick building among the Thracians at a comparatively early epoch marks an important moment in the development of architecture in Thrace. Real brick building in the Hellenistic age first appeared in the Eastern Hellenistic states of Mesopotamia, Syria, etc. In Greece bricks appeared only sporadically as building material in the fourth to third century, and not in whole buildings at that.[34] It is apparent from the studies made so far of the art of building in Magna Graecia and Italy that there, too, bricks appeared very late — barely in the third century B.C. in Magna Graecia, and in Italy at the turn of the second and first century B.C. while in Rome brick construction was quite unfamiliar up to the Imperial epoch.

In the construction of Greece and the Greek colonies stone and sun-dried bricks were the basic building materials in the pre-Roman period.[35]

Without thinking that the question of the appearance of bricks in Thrace can be finally solved and without wanting to minimize the importance of the existence of close mutual cultural influences between Thrace and the Hellenistic East in its early period, we consider that the development of local building traditions should, above all, be borne in mind. On the basis of the fact that the Thracians made wide use of sun-dried bricks as building material, we consider that in the frequent fires which occurred they would have been able to discover the stability and advantages of baked bricks. They were thus easily able, and by independent means to reach the discovery and use of bricks in such construction which, in their structure and plan, like that of the beehive tombs, required more resistant material to support the heavy load of the high mounds of earth.

The brick tombs of Seuthopolis and the brick tomb with frescoes near Kazanluk, dated to the end of the fourth and the early third century B.C., and near Muglizh, dated to the end of the third century B.C., provide evidence that a school of architecture and painting existed in the region around Seuthopolis, which created highly artistic monuments of the Early Hellenistic art of construction and painting.

Minor Arts. Finds of iron chisels and other tools for stone-working prove that stone-cutting closely linked with the needs of construction was well developed in Seuthopolis. Local granite from the Sredna Gora Mountains was used in making the architectural details. Various weapons were also found in the course of the diggings. The curved knives, known from fourth century B.C. Thracian burials, were of special interest. The arrow tips were three-edged, like the Scythian arrows, and were made of bronze (Fig. 55). These articles were made locally and provide evidence of well-developed iron-working and bronze casting.

The markedly developed taste of the Thracians for jewellery and plaques, serving to adorn men or horses, made it imperative to develop the extensive production of small artistic works of silver, gold and bronze, in which we see characteristic Thracian forms: fibulae, earrings, and rings.

About 80 fibulae of the so-called Thracian type, characteristic of the lands inhabited by the Thracians, were found at the diggings of Seuthopolis.[36] They had an arc-shaped bow with a single-sided spiral at their back end. The pin holder was formed in several ways: either curving backward, parallel to the bow, or continuing upward and ending with a small cone-shaped ball. These fibulae show different variants of the Thracian-type fibulae and outline their development (Fig. 56). Together with them were found another 30 fibulae which also have an arc-shaped bow like the Thracian fibulae, but have a bilateral spiral; they demonstrate the La Tène influence in Seuthopolis, resulting from contacts with the Celts and their culture.

A bronze plaque made in the animal style is a characteristic work of the local Thracian jewellers' craft.

Two snakes, made of lead, should be mentioned as the work of local metal working. They are curled in three spirals with erect heads. They have small elliptical pits on top, imitating snakeskin, and the horizontal furrows of a snake's body are indicated below by schematically indicated incised lines (Fig. 57).

In Seuthopolis local traditions were soundly observed, alongside the extensive penetration of Hellenistic artistic forms and conceptions. An architectural terracotta, probably an antefix, depicting a man's head, which has nothing in common with Hellenistic aesthetic principles, is a striking example of this. The traits of the face are most laconically, almost conventionally treated, yet an original expressiveness has been achieved in spite of this (Fig. 65).

The archaeological material from Seuthopolis offers a rich combination of Thracian traditions with elements of Hellenistic culture and are evidence of the high level of cultural development attained by part of Thracian society in the Early Hellenistic Age.

3. COMMERCE

Seuthopolis was more than an important centre around which workshops for industrial activity were concentrated. Part of its inhabitants and persons living here, probably Greek settlers, were engaged in commerce. Expensive goods were imported for the needs of the affluent stratum of the population: beautiful vessels made of clay and metal, gold jewellery and other luxury goods, olive oil and wine. Amphorae with pointed bottoms were used to transport wine and olive oil. Many sherds of the bottoms, mouths and handles of such vessels were found in the process of digging in the city, and in the earth of the mounds at the necropolis, while several whole amphorae were found in the burials of Tumuli 1 and 2. All have the form typical of the Thasos amphorae of the turn of the fourth and third century B.C. The amphora stamps provide evidence of the close links with the Island of Thasos, since of a total of about 90 stamps, two-thirds came from Thasos.[37] The main group of Thasos stamps are rectangular in form, a characteristic form for the Hellenistic age, with the emblem in the centre and the inscription containing the Ethnikon and the personal name (Fig. 58). The most frequently met names are: Ἀριστοφάνης, Κράτινος, Παμφάης etc. The emblems show a variety of pictures — of fruit (olives, grapes, pomegranates, etc.), vessels (amphorae, krateroi, etc.), cult symbols (the double axe, trident, lyre, bukrainion, horns of plenty, etc.).

In one group of Thasos stamps various letters are met with instead of emblems: A, B, Γ, Δ, E, H, Λ, M, P, Ϛ and the name Πολυνείκης. Several stamps, representing individual letters or monograms of several letters and stamped on with round or rectangular dies, can also be considered as Thasos amphora stamps. Several examples of a 'wheel-like' form, depicting a wheel divided by spokes into 3, 4 or 5 sections in each of which a letter has been placed, also belong to the group of stamps with monograms.

Several stamps are from Sinope, and from unknown centres.

Greek Pottery. A considerable number of vessels and a large quantity of sherds of Greek black glaze pottery were found at the Seuthopolis dig and in its necropolis.[38] Found during regular digging at the site of a Thracian city, the Greek pottery of Seuthopolis is an important source for the economic history of the city and of the Thracian Hinterland along the upper reaches of the Toundja and the Maritsa.

About 3000 sherds of black glaze vessels were found in Seuthopolis. Of them about one third, 1000 sherds, were from kantharoi, 1000 are the bottoms and walls of vessels whose form cannot be determined; 350 sherds are from dishes and small bowls, 200 from fish plates, 50 from lekythoi and 30 sherds from lamps.

The group of the kantharoi is the most numerous. An insignificant fraction, about ten sherds from Kantharoi, chiefly found in the earth of Tumulus No 1 and Tumulus No 2, has a rounded mouth slightly curved outward, under the rim of which a ring in relief has been formed, often having a triangular cross-section. Similar rings are found on the kantharoi of Type III in Apollonia, which are dated to the second half of the fourth century. However, this type began to be used in the early years of the fourth century, as can be concluded from the material found at Olynthus and on the Island of Thasos.[39]

All the remaining kantharoi found in Seuthopolis belong to Type IV or to Variant A of the same type in Apollonia (Fig. 59).

They have a high slender body. The relation between the cylindrical neck and the semi-spherical body is almost proportional.[40] They are made of fine, finely sieved clay which acquired a light brick red colour after baking. The kantharoi are covered inside and outside with a black glaze, which in some of them is brown in colour.

The closest parallels to the kantharoi of Seuthopolis are to be found in the materials from the Athenian agora, Group A,[41] from an Athenian necropolis and other finds in Greece, dated to the turn of the fourth and third century B.C. Their Attic origin is indisputable. This type of kantharoi were also wide-spread in the towns of the Northern Black Sea coastal strip.[42]

Garlands of laurel or ivy leaves placed additionally on the slip with diluted clay, i.e. the barbotine technique, is found on the necks of smooth and grooved kantharoi. The garlands are usually single, but in some cases twigs branched off from the main twig (Fig. 60). In only one sherd was another motif found — probably an ear of wheat.

This type of ornamentation is characteristic of Early Hellenistic pottery of the turn of the fourth and third century B.C. A considerable number of black glaze vessels with ornaments of this kind were found in the digging at the foot of the West Slope of the Acropolis. Later diggings in Athens increased their number, and confirmed the thesis of their Attic origin. However, whereas in the Athenian samples white paint and gold is often found, only diluted clay is used in the material from Seuthopolis. There may also have been gilding which was rubbed off.

28

Ornamentation in relief, placed chiefly on the handles, also appears alongside with this ornamentation on the kantharoi. We have three handles from Seuthopolis with this type of ornamentation. On two of them, a projection in relief in the form of a mask with a wide-open mouth, had been stuck onto the curve, while in the third there was an ivy leaf.

Graffiti were scratched onto several kantharos handles: ΔI , K, H. The graffiti are found on the under side of the small stands BI, K, Χ or on the neck — KEP. (Fig. 61).

Only one sherd of a skyphos with red-figure decoration was found in Seuthopolis. Part of the palmettes only was preserved. The considerably narrowed part of the vessel, placed on a small ring-like stand, brings the sherd found in Seuthopolis close to skyphos No 487 from Apollonia, dated to the second quarter of the fourth century B. C. and attributed to the Kerch style of Attic vases.

Sherds of dishes and small bowls, extensively used in Seuthopolis, are second in number. All are made of finely washed and sieved clay which acquired a light brick-red colour after baking. Entirely covered with black glaze, the bottom underneath has been left the colour of the clay and on it narrower and wider rings of black slip have been applied.

Part of the dishes and small bowls are ornamented on the inside of the base with stamped palmettes, placed in a circle and connected with incised interlacing arcs. This motif was already well known in the fifth century, but was widespread in the fourth and the first half of the third century.

Graffiti were found on a large number of the small bowls: ΦIΛAI , ΔIK , NOY , etc.

Numerous sherds of fish plates prove that this type of vessel was also extensively used in Seuthopolis. They are broad, shallow and slightly inclined towards the centre, where there is a semi-spherical hollow. A broad border drops almost perpendicularly from the edge. The base is a ring-shaped stand, like that on ordinary dishes. The fish plates are usually entirely covered with black glaze. Sometimes the bases are left the colour of the clay, or are covered with a slip on which narrow or broader concentric bands of black glaze have been placed. The fish plates of Olynthus, Thasos, Samos and Olbia are close in type, being of Attic origin and dated to the second half of the fourth century. The dishes from Seuthopolis are dated to the same period.

Graffiti have been scratched onto a large number of bases. Only three whole names have been written out: ΕΡΗ , ΔI and APIΞΕNOϹ . ΕΡI and ΔI are consecrations to Hera and Zeus, while APIΞΕNOϹ was probably the name of the owner of the plate. Most of the individual letters should also be connected with the names of owners. The two H are of a more special character, horizontally and vertically written in the same way as on the amphora stamps IH.

The black glaze fish plates were soon widespread among the inhabitants of Seuthopolis, and also began to be imitated by the Thracian potters, as proved by the large number of sherds of fish plates made of grey or red clay.

Although considerably fewer in number compared with the kantharoi and fish plates, the lekythoi from Seuthopolis show that this Greek vessel was also known here.

An Aryballos-shaped lekythos had been placed in the burial in Tumulus No 1. The net-like ornament covering the body and the stand is comparatively rare, and has white dots carefully placed at the crossing points. Masses of aryballos-shaped lekythoi were found in the necropolis of Apollonia, where they were dated to the end of the second quarter of the fourth century to the early years of the third century B.C. The fact that only one aryballos-shaped lekythos was found in Seuthopolis and in the earliest burial at that makes us consider that its use must have been more restricted here, only up to the end of the fourth century B.C.

Lacrimaria were found in the burials of Tumuli Nos 1 and 2, as well as in the city, which shows that these vessels were used in daily life in Seuthopolis.

They were made of fine, or badly sieved clay which acquired an ochre or brick-red colour after baking. These vessels, which have thicker or thinner walls, were not covered with slip, but some of them had red painted bands. Their bodies are blown out in an egg shape, widest at the shoulders. In form the lacrimaria from Seuthopolis are closest to type II from Apollonia. The lacrimaria from Athens, Thasos and the Northern Black Sea colonies of the turn of the fourth and third century B.C. are closest in form to those of Seuthopolis.

Twelve whole lamps and many sherds of these vessels were found, two of the lamps coming to light in burials, two in the earth of Tumulus No 2 and the remainder in the city. They all had one wick and belong to various groups of Howland's Type 25[43] (Fig. 62).

Five lamps and three sherds belong to Type 25 A, characterized by high rounded walls of the reservoir, separated from the border by a deep groove, surrounding the mouth, through which the oil was poured. The lamps of this type found in the Athenian agora are dated to the second quarter of the fourth century up to the first quarter of the third century. Several of the lamps grouped in Type I from Apollonia and dated to the same period, are of this type. They are covered with black glaze inside and out, with the exception of the lower side of the bottom.

Six lamps belong to Howland's Type 25 AI. This variant is quite close to the former one, but the lamps are not glazed. Moreover, some of them have a longer body, and the border around the central opening is modelled with greater variety.

One lamp can be linked with Type 25 B. The difference between this group and 25 A consists chiefly in that there is a protuberance on the left side of the lamp.

About ten sherds of small bowls and of the walls of other vessels made of fine clay, and ornamented with horizontal bands in red were found in Seuthopolis. This pottery should be linked with the Rhodian and Ionian pottery widespread in the Ionian centres as early as the Archaic period, and which continued to be produced later. The fine quality of the clay leaves no doubt that this was no local imitation, but imported from a centre in Asia Minor, even though in very limited amounts.

However, the predominant quantity of Greek pottery found in Seuthopolis was of Attic origin and belongs to the last quarter of the fourth century and the first quarter of the third century B.C. Only a few of the sherds belong to an earlier period: one from a black-figure lekythos of the second half of the fifth century B.C., sherds of a red-figure skyphos, of a pyxis, of an aryballos-shaped lekythos and a lamp which are dated to the first half of the fourth century. All the remaining vessels show characteristic features of the Attic pottery of the Early Hellenistic age in form, technique and ornamentation. The extensive use of Greek vessels in Seuthopolis, such as kantharoi, fish plates, small bowls, lamps, etc., and the mass imitation of their forms by the Thracian potters are evidence of the increasing penetration of Greek forms in the way of life of Thracian society. The use of lacrimaria, aryballos-shaped lekythoi and lamps in the tombs show that this influence was not restricted to daily life alone, but was also reflected in burial customs.

The abundance of Greek words and letters scratched onto the vessels is of special interest. Although they do not give us any data of a historical nature or more information on onomastics and religion, the graffiti are proof of a good knowledge of Greek in Seuthopolis, which is supported by the presence of graffiti on the pithoi and on vessels and sherds of local pottery.

Lastly, the Greek pottery from Seuthopolis eloquently shows the great scope of the city's commercial relations with Athens in the Early Hellenistic age. In that period, owing to the fact that the East was drawn into the system of the ancient economy, commerce flourished very greatly and was accompanied by a great development of industry. This process of an economic advance, observed in a number of cities in Greece, Asia Minor and Egypt in the course of the third century B.C., undoubtedly began as early as the reign of Alexander of Macedon. The creation of new trade and industrial centres in the extensive Hellenistic monarchies and of new trade routes, led to a decline in the economic importance of certain Greek cities. However, Athens succeeded in adapting herself to the new conditions, and at the turn of the fourth and the third century began to produce large quantities of black glaze pottery vessels, the characteristic feature of which was no longer red-figure decoration, but stamped ornaments, barbotine decoration and ornamentation in relief. The Attic pottery of that time is found in many cities in Italy, Egypt, Syria, Palestine, Phoenicia, etc. However, a considerable part of Athenian exports were intended for the Northern Black Sea shores and the Western Black Sea colonies with their Hinterland, which remained the principal producer of wheat for Athens.[44] Thrace was a good market for Athenian goods from the beginning of the fifth century B.C. and Athens preserved her economic influence here throughout the whole of the fourth and the first half of the third century B.C. in the reigns of Philip II, Alexander III and Lysimachus, as is convincingly proved by the newly-found pottery material from Seuthopolis. It completes the general picture of the trade relations of Athens in the Early Hellenistic age, which were sound and regular with the colonies along the Western Black Sea coast, above all with Apollonia, and also with the Thracian Hinterland.

The extensive penetration of Greek goods in Seuthopolis was facilitated by the Black Sea colonies along the present-day Bulgarian coast. However, the natural waterways — the Rivers Hebros (Maritsa) and Tonsos (Toundja), which were far deeper in Antiquity — were of no less importance. Navigable over the larger part of their length, they secured direct contact with the islands and the cities along the Aegean coast.

Seuthopolis maintained particularly close relations in the sphere of art with Athens, one of the large Greek centres of art, and this had a most favourable effect on the development of the local culture. Of course, the Greek influence affected, above all, the way of life and the culture of the affluent class, which alone had the economic possibility of building spacious dwellings and decorating them richly, as well as building monumental tombs, and obtaining expensive works of art and of the art crafts. Sculptures were the least numerous among the works of art. Only a few fragments of marble statues and reliefs were found in the city: the head of a young man (Fig. 63), the wings of an eagle or a winged sphinx, and the head of a panther, which may have been parts of larger groups of statuary or compositions in relief. All these fragments show fine workmanship and a subtle artistic taste in the style of Greek art. The inhabitants of Seuthopolis showed a marked preference for clay statuettes and terracottas, the production of which flourished greatly in the Hellenistic age. The figurines of graceful maidens with delicate faces, wrapped in himations which fell in graceful folds, found in Seuthopolis together with various deities of the Greek Pantheon — Eros, Cybele, etc. — are of the Tanagra type in style and most of them were imported (Fig. 64). The rich gifts from the necropolis of Seuthopolis — the gilded bronze situla, tray and oinochoe and the silver kylix, are evidence of connections with a large Greek bronze-casting centre. Part of the funeral gold jewellery, necklaces and earrings, found in the burials, can be considered as the work of Hellenistic goldsmiths.

All these finds are evidence that the Hellenistic traditions of art were the form of official art, and also met the aesthetic requirements of the inhabitants of Seuthopolis.

CHAPTER III

MONEY CIRCULATION IN SEUTHOPOLIS
AND THE MINT OF SEUTHES III

Ancient Coins from Seuthopolis

Alongside the other archaeological material, the coins found during digging at Seuthopolis illustrate the prosperity of this ancient city in the years of its existence. About 1200 ancient coins were found in the city, part minted by the local Dynast Seuthes III (843 coins) and the rest minted in a great variety of centres and other rulers of the ancient world, and chiefly by the Macedonian Kings Philip II and Alexander the Great.

The absolute chronological limits of Seuthopolis as an inhabited locality were established thanks to the coins — the earliest are coins struck by Philip II of Macedon (359-336 B.C.), and the latest several coins attributed either to Demetrius II (239-229 B.C.) or to Demetrius I (306-283 B.C.).

The Greek colonies along the Thracian Black Sea and Aegean areas are represented by comparatively poor numismatic material. Only two bronze coins were found from Mesambria, depicting on the obverse a helmet full face, while the reverse has a wheel with rays and four spokes, and the inscription M E T A. From Apollonia there comes a silver coin with a head of Apollo and an anchor turned upwards. A bronze coin from Aegospotami, on which there is a head of Demeter and a goat facing left, represents the production of that city. A lion breaking a spear and again the head of Demeter are engraved on a bronze coin from Cardia. In 309 B.C. Lysimachus built his capital at this city, and gave it his own name, Lysimachia. About ten bronze coins from Lysimachia, similar to the coins of Lysimachus, were found in Seuthopolis, showing the veiled head of Demeter and a wreath of ears of wheat, the head of Tyche and a lion seated to the right, the head of a lion, and again an ear of wheat. Aenus is represented by bronze coins on which there is the head of Hermes with a petasos, typical of the city, and a goat standing to the right. The second type shows the head of a beardless man with a laurel wreath and a caduceus, on both sides of which the city's name is written. A bronze coin with the head of Apollo and a helmet with dropped cheek-pieces comes from Orthagoria, while two bronze coins with the head of Herakles, covered with a lion skin, and a tripod on the reverse, come from Philippi. Athens, the centre of the classical world, has sent only one silver tetradrachm with the inevitable helmeted head of Athene and her owl, to Seuthopolis. The lack of coins from this city is quite unexpected when it is borne in mind that the royal court of the Kingdom of Seuthes maintained active political relations with Athens, where the Thracian kings were also valued, and particularly Seuthes III as a natural ally against the Macedonians. Nevertheless, this lack can be explained up to a point by the abundance of

Attic pottery in Seuthopolis. Obviously Athens realized a large part of her commerce with the Thracians by the export of high grade and artistically worked vessels. It can be considered that of the listed centres only Lysimachia was in more permanent economic relations with Seuthopolis. The remaining cities most probably lay outside its traditional commercial routes, and their coins happened to reach Seuthopolis after prolonged wanderings over the markets of the ancient world. In contrast to them the coins of the Macedonian kings from Philip II to Cassander circulated intensively in the city, as well as those of Lysimachus, the Satrap of Thrace after the death of Alexander the Great. These coins bore the brunt of the circulation of coins in Seuthopolis, particularly before the considerable development of local minting at the end of the fourth century B.C.

Philip II is represented by several silver tetradrachms with the head of Zeus and a horseman. One of them has a bronze centre and a silver-plated surface, the usual weight of the silver tetradrachms struck according to the Attic standard, about 17 grams, being preserved. About 100 of this king's bronze coins were found in Seuthopolis, with the head of a young man and a horseman riding to the left, the head of a young man and a horseman jumping to the right or left, the head of Herakles with the lion skin, and a horseman jumping to the right. The silver coins of Alexander the Great have two nominal values: tetradrachms (4) and drachms (about 20). The designs are one and the same for both values: the head of the young Herakles with the lion skin, and Zeus, seated on a throne with eagle and sceptre (Fig. 66). There are several tens of bronze coins of Alexander, of 10 types. The most characteristic of them have a head of Herakles and a quiver, a bow and quiver or club and a bow-case in various positions, a head of Apollo and a horseman galloping to the right.

The varied supplementary symbols and monograms on the coins of these two rulers indicate the various centres of the vast Macedonian Empire in which they were struck, and in some of the silver coins more particularly betray their posthumous character. For the time being the cities identified are Pella, Priene and Lampsacus.

Three silver drachms of Philip III Arridaeus (323-316 B.C.) have been preserved, whose types repeat the silver coins of Alexander the Great already described. The bronze coins of Philip III are also similar to those of Alexander: a head of Apollo and a horseman jumping to the right. Here the initials ΛΥ under the inscription are interesting.

These initials show that the bronze coins were struck by Lysimachus, as the deputy of Philip III. The same feature is to be seen on the only bronze coin of Alexander IV (323-311 B.C.), depicting the head of a young man and a horseman jumping to the right.

Under Cassander a great increase in the number of bronze coins struck by this ruler is again to be observed. There were about 50 of them. There are good grounds to consider that after the death of Philip II and Alexander the Great, the coins of Cassander were the most wide-spread foreign coins in Seuthopolis, but they no longer held the predominant place on the local market, being displaced by the coins of Seuthes III. A large part of the coins of Cassander which made their way to Seuthopolis were used as raw material by the local mint, about 80 of the coins of Seuthes being overstruck on Cassander's.

Cassander's coins depicted the head of Herakles with a lion skin and a lion couchant or a horseman riding to the right, or the head of Apollo and a tripod.

Several anonymous bronze coins with a Macedonian shield and a tall Macedonian helmet with dropped cheek-pieces also belong with representatives of Macedonian minting.

Hitherto, the six bronze coins of Demetrius II (239-229 B.C.) were considered the latest, having the Macedonian shield and the monogram of the royal name, and with the Macedonian helmet on the reverse. According to A. T. Newell, however, the coins of this type should be attributed to Demetrius I (306-283 B.C.). The Syrian dynasts are represented by two coins. One of them, the tetradrachm of Seleucus I (312-280 B.C.) again repeats the already familiar silver coins of Alexander the Great, but here Zeus is holding Nike in his outstretched hand. The second is a bronze coin struck by Antiochus (281-261 B.C.). A portrait of the ruler is engraved on the obverse and a tripod on the reverse.

Lysimachus (316-281 B.C.) depicts the portrait of deified Alexander the Great on his tetradrachms on the obverse and seated Athene holding a Victory on the reverse. Two such coins were found at Seuthopolis (Fig. 66). One of them was struck in Pergamum. His three types of bronze coins number about 40. They depict the head of Athene and a jumping lion, the head of Herakles with a lion skin and wreath of ears of wheat, and the head of a young man with a Phrygian helmet and a trophy, piled over with arms. The extremely warlike appearance of the latter type connects it with Lysimachus' victory at Ipsus in 301 B.C.[45]

Fourteen bronze coins with the head of Apollo and a tripod, the head of Herakles and a club, and the head of a boar and a spearhead, are attributed to the minting of Adaios, a dynast known only from his coins.[46]

In conclusion mention should be made of two completely unknown coins of Thracian rulers, found in Seuthopolis, which will probably provide the occasion for the discovery of new pages in Thracian history.

More than 800 bronze coins of different values struck by Seuthes III were found in Seuthopolis. In quantity they are considerably more numerous than the foreign coins, which indicates the definite economic role of local minting. They are greatly depended on, since they offer a complete picture of the minting of Seuthes III. This gives great opportunities for establishing the relative, and in general lines the absolute chronology of the individual types of coins. The successful overcoming of this great question mark in numismatics will place the key to many problems in the hands of historians, problems concerning Early Hellenistic society among the Thracians and the organization of their state. That is why exceptional attention is paid to the Thracian coins from Seuthopolis, and great hopes are placed upon them.

The coins of Seuthes are grouped in 7 main types:

1. obv. Head of Zeus with a laurel wreath or diadem to the right.

   rev. Spearhead to the right. Above it ΣΕΥΘΟΥ. Below it a symbol-star with a different number of points. 20 coins (Fig. 67a).

2. obv. Head of Zeus with laurel wreath to right.

   rev. Thunderbolt, above it ΣΕΥΘΟΥ . Below it a symbol-star with a different number of points or a wreath. 30 coins (Fig. 67b).

3. obv. Eight-point star. Circle of grains.

   rev. Thunderbolt, above it ΣΕΥΘΟΥ . 67 coins (Fig. 67c).

4. obv. Eagle with folded wings to right. Circle of grains.

   rev. Wreath of ears of a cereal in the middle $\frac{ΣΕΥ}{ΘΟΥ}$. 106 coins (Fig. 67d).

5. obv. Eagle with folded wings to right. With or without circle of grain.

   rev. Thunderbolt, above it ΣΕΥΘΟΥ . 38 coins (Fig. 68).

6. obv. Head of Zeus with laurel wreath to right. With or without circle of grain.

   rev. Horse moving slowly right above it ΣΕΥΘΟΥ . Below symbol-star with varying number of points, a wreath or a star and wreath together. In some cases symbols are lacking. 293 coins (Fig. 69).

7. obv. Head of a bearded man with long hair and laurel wreath to right. Portrait of Seuthes III. With or without circle of grains.

   rev. Horsman jumping to right. Above it ΣΕΥΘΟΥ . Below symbols — wreath or eight-point star. In some cases symbols are lacking. 287 coins (Fig. 70).

Type 1 is only known from Seuthopolis. It is attributed to the minting of Seuthes III, and not to any of the other Thracian kings of that name because of the following considerations:

The chronological limits of ancient Seuthopolis are fixed by the coins of Philip II and those of Demetrius II or Demetrius I. Only one Seuthes, Seuthes III, is known within this chronological framework. The designs on this type are thematically similar to those on five of the remaining 6 types of coins minted by Seuthes III. On them either the image of Zeus or one of his attributes, is to be found: a thunderbolt, an eagle, and in the present case a spear.

The image of Zeus on this type is, in general lines, analogous with Zeus on the coins of Philip II, and also with Zeus on types 2 and 6. The resemblance is expressed in the similar manner of treating the individual elements: straight nose, curly beard, clearly marked laurel wreath.

The spearhead is also found on the coins of Cassander (316-297 B. C.).

The symbol-star with a varying number of points is also characteristic of the coins of Cassander, as well as of the three other types of Seuthes — 2, 6 and 7.

Many scholars attributed some of the types thus listed (most often those with the eagle) to the minting of Seuthes IV (about 200 B. C.). This point of view was categorically disproved by the Seuthopolis numismatic material in which all seven types, according to stratigraphy, themes of the representations and inscriptions are components of one and the same minting — that of Seuthes III.

The coins of Seuthes overstruck on older foreign coins are of particular interest and importance. There are about 90 of them.

What can be said about the dating and chronology of Seuthes' coins?

Up to the present time the extensive research work devoted to them was based without exception on stylistic analysis and overstriking. Owing to lack of material from archaeological diggings, no stratigraphic data are quoted. Two scanty hoards of Seuthes' coins, which nevertheless existed, were neglected quite without justification.

At the present moment our conclusions can be based on several points.

1. The types on the coins of Seuthes mark two large thematic groups: A (Types 1-6 incl.) whose designs are entirely in the spirit of the cult of Zeus, and B (Type 7), in which the cult of King Seuthes III himself is reflected. For its part, Group A is divided into two sub-groups — A I and A II. Only the attributes of Zeus (the thunderbolt and the eagle with folded wings) are depicted on the coins of A I (Types 3, 4 and 5), while on those of A II (Types 1, 2 and 6) the image of the deity is to be seen. In our opinion these three groups represent individual stages of the minting of Seuthes III and should be delimited both thematically and chronologically.

It is of interest to note that the cult of Zeus is not typical of the Thracian religion and was not reflected on the Thracian coins preceding Seuthes III. In this respect the latter's minting was quite a new event. Macedonian elements are much more clearly to be discovered in it than those of the ancient Thracian traditions. This phenomenon was probably the result of the great advance of Hellenic influence after the campaigns of Philip II in Thrace.

2. The accessory symbols on Seuthes' coins again group them in sections — with and without symbols. In the first we find A II and B of the above item, and in the second — A I. From this it can be concluded that A II and B are found with the same symbols, although with varying frequency: in Type 1 only a star, in Type 2 a star and a wreath, in type 6 the star predominates and the wreath is seen far less (they are also found together), and in Type 7 only the wreath is found and the star in two cases alone.

3. The overstruck coins can already provide a more exact idea for the dating of the individual types. This is how they are distributed:

Type 4 — 1 on coin of unidentified type;

Type 5 — 3 on coins of Cassander with a couchant lion (316-306 B.C.);

Type 6 — 3 on coins of Alexander, 17 on Cassander's with a lion, 1 on Cassander's with a tripod (306-305 B.C.), 3 on Cassander's with a horseman (301 B.C.)[47], 1 on a coin of Lysimachus, of an uncertain type, and 45 undefined overstrikes.

Type 7 — 2 on Cassander's coins with a lion, 2 on Cassander's coins with a tripod, 4 on Cassander's coins with a horseman, and 6 undefined.

It is obvious that Types 6 and 7 are the latest. They were also struck after 306 B.C. According to the above overstrikes the conclusion can be drawn that they were minted almost simultaneously. However, the different symbols (see Item 2) indicate the contrary. Besides, both types are represented by a very large number of coins — they were struck for the needs of circulation, which could hardly have occurred in a definite period by the simultaneous circulation of a vast number of coins of both types, vast by the scale of Seuthes' minting. Moreover, the number of overstruck coins of both types is quite different. This indicates that they were struck under different conditions of the milieu of circulation in the region of Seuthopolis — Type 6, when the coins of Cassander and Lysimachus were to be found in abundance, and Type 7 either before or after this period. However, as was seen, some of the overstruck coins date Type 7 after 306 B.C., so that it has to be accepted that this type was struck after Type 6. This conclusion is particularly clearly confirmed by the distribution of the two types.

It is far more logical to place Type 5 before Type 6, because overstriking on coins struck only before 306 B.C. is found. Their small number is an indication that this type ceased to be struck before the coins of Cassander made their way on a large scale into Seuthopolis. In this way, dating by way of orientation can be given to Type 5, with a final limit of about 313-310 B.C. For Type 7 it can be allowed that the time when it was first struck coincided with the years immediately after the death of Cassander (297 B.C.) which put an end to the largest source of foreign coins in Seuthopolis in the last 15 years of the fourth century, representatives of the last issues of this king remaining in circulation.

However, if Type 7 is dated later than Type 6 does not the lack of overstriking of this type on coins of Cassander and Lysimachus appear as an argument against this?

It is known that after 301 B.C. (the Battle of Ipsus), Lysimachus settled chiefly in Asia Minor. This should have led to a reduction of his coins in Thrace, chiefly of the bronze coins which were intended for more local use. And indeed, only 5 of Lysimachus' coins with trophies come from Seuthopolis out of a total of 40 bronze coins of this ruler. As to Cassander's coins with a horseman, owing to the similarity of the types with Type 7 (also a horseman, only not galloping) it would be rather difficult to establish the type of the old coin in overstriking of Type 7 on such a coin. Several overstruck examples of Type 7 arouse the suspicion that it was precisely the coins of Cassander with a horseman which were used to this end.

The only coin of Type 4 which shows slight traces of having been overstruck cannot give grounds for firmer conclusions as to the dating of this type. It was one of the 'large' types, represented by 106 coins and the presence of only one overstrike, not very certain at that, shows that the type was struck under conditions in which overstriking was not so necessary as for types 5, 6 and 7. This could well have been the period at the end of the reign of Alexander the Great, or immediately after his death, when his bronze coins, and probably also those of Philip II, were valued and preferred in payment, so that it was not necessary to overstrike them. Moreover, it is logical to suppose that when he first began to mint money Seuthes III felt no insufficiency of material for his coins.

It should be noted that the above coin appears in a way as a connecting link between Types 4 and 5. First the form of the coin (with a larger diameter and flatter) is characteristic of Type 5, not of Type 4. Second, the eagle on this coin has a marked tail, slightly outspread, which is much closer to that of the eagles on Type 5. Owing to these considerations the two types should be taken as 'neighbours' in the minting of Seuthes, Type 4 being the earlier of the two.

4. Stratigraphy and Distribution of Seuthes' Coins. According to their distribution the monetary types of Seuthes III can be grouped as follows:

— distributed only in the city (Type 1).

— in the city and the earth of the three tumuli (Types 2, 3, 4, 5, 6).

— in the city and the tombs of the tumuli (Type 7).

This method of grouping confirms the fact that Type 7 is the latest, since it is found in the tombs but is not found in the earth of the tumuli. All the materials contained in the latter chronologically precede those in the tombs. A certain period of the minting and circulation of Type 7 coincides with a new stage in the development of the funeral furniture in Seuthopolis — the appearance of the rectangular brick tombs instead of the older beehive ones. A small hoard of 4 coins with the portrait of Seuthes came to light in one of the two secondary brick tombs with rectangular plan in Tumulus No 2. Is is interesting to note that gold fibulae showing a Celtic influence were found in the other tomb, and this categorically dates the tombs after the year 300 B. C.

The stratigraphy of the individual types in the city also confirms the fact that Types 6 and 7 were the latest:

TABLE 1

Stratigraphy of Coins Found in the City

Depth	Type 1	Type 2	Type 3	Type 4	Type 5	Type 6	Type 7
0-0.20 m	2(10%)	1(4%)	4(6%)	5(5%)	2(6%)	10(3%)	11(4%)
0.20-0.40 m		1(4%)	5(8%)	10(11%)	5(16%)	32(11%)	52(20%)
0.40-0.60 m	4(21%)	6(25%)	13(20%)	20(22%)	6(19%)	98(35%)	85(33%)
0.60-0.80 m	4(21%)	7(29%)	22(35%)	28(30%)	13(42%)	78(28%)	69(27%)
0.80-1.00 m	6(32%)	4(17%)	13(20%)	19(21%)	4(13%)	36(16%)	32(12%)
1.00-1.20 m	2(10%)	5(20%)	4(6%)	7(8%)	1(3%)	14(5%)	9(4%)
1.20-1.40 m	1(5%)			3(3%)		5(2%)	
1.40-1.60 m			1(2%)			1	
Total	19	24	62	92	31	274	257

5. <u>Weight of the Coins</u>. Here the average weight and limits of the predominant weights of coins of every type are established. The results are as follows:

<u>Type 1</u> - average weight 1.29 g; predominant weights between 1.01 and 1.40 g.
<u>Type 2</u> - average weight 2.50 g; predominant weights between 2.01 and 2.60 g.
<u>Type 3</u> - average weight 1.59 g; predominant weights between 1.21 and 1.60 g.
<u>Type 4</u> - average weight 2.96 g; predominant weights between 2.81 and 3.20 g.
<u>Type 5</u> - average weight 3.66 g; predominant weights between 3.01 and 3.80 g.
<u>Type 6</u> - average weight 4.51 g; predominant weights between 3.21 and 4.00 g.
                          4.21 and 4.40 g.
                          5.41 and 5.60 g.
<u>Type 7</u> - average weight 5.61 g; predominant weights between 5.41 and 6.40 g.

The bronze of which the coins were struck was not highly valued and the difference of several grammes in coins of one and the same type was frequent. The table shows that in types 1 - 5 and 7 the average weight fits into the limits of predominant weights. In Type 6, however, these limits are very wide and are not compact — a reduction in the number of coins with weights between 4.00-4.20 and 4.40-5.40 g is to be observed. We are inclined to explain this anomaly by the large amount of overstriking which led to a great variety in the weight of the coins. Also bearing in mind the hoards containing coins of Type 6 precisely, we consider that this type was struck under the conditions of most intensive circulation. These conditions imposed the rapid introduction of new quantities of coins into circulation, which led to negligence in striking them as regards their weight.

A curious detail has also been established — the coins of Types 6 and 7 struck from the same dies (with few exceptions) have very similar weights (within the limits of 0.60-0.80 g). Obviously the weights of the coins depended on the personal feeling of the moneyers for weight. The possibility that certain of Seuthes' monetary types of smaller weight were subdivisions of the larger ones and that at a particular period they were in circulation instead of them is not to be excluded. In this respect Group A II (Types 1, 2 and 6) arouses the greatest suspicions. As was noted, Type 6, which is the principal one both in weight and in the number of coins, was in use under the conditions of intensive circulation, in which coins of lower values would have been necessary. However, nothing can as yet be said with certainty about this question.

6. <u>Hoards of Seuthes' Coins</u>. Two such hoards originate from Seuthopolis, increasing the total number known with coins of Seuthes to four.

The first hoard consists of four coins of Type 7, found in the brick tomb 3 in tumulus No 2. One of them is overstruck on one of Cassander's coins with a tripod.

The second hoard contains 21 coins of Type 6 (7 overstruck, 2 of which on Cassander's lion and one on one of Alexander's coins) and a coin of Cassander with a lion couchant.

The composition of the two hoards confirms the fact that Types 6 and 7 were not in circulation at the same time.

The first hoard is of a more special character — it was found in the tomb in which it was a funeral gift. In this same tomb 3 a silver drachm of Alexander the Great was found. Four of the coins of Type 7 were worn which is why there are no grounds to place the time when they were struck close to the time when they were placed in the tomb. It should therefore be accepted that, since the brick tombs of a rectangular plan are the latest stage of funeral construction near Seuthopolis, Type 7 had been struck earlier than the time of the use of the tombs, but some examples of this type were still in circulation in Seuthopolis. The second hoard provides several valuable data on the circulation of Type 6. The depth at which it was found, (55 cm) above all corresponds to the stratum of 40-60 cm, in which there was the largest number of coins of Types 6 and 7, and this supports the correctness of the conclusions drawn from our stratigraphic observations concerning these types. All the coins of the hoard were out of circulation before 306 B.C., since the foreign coin (Cassander's) was dated between 316 and 306 B.C., and the overstrikes identified are on coins of the same type. The coexistence of overstruck and regular foreign coins in the hoard emphasizes the fact that overstriking was chiefly dictated by the need for material for the local mint. However, certain directing influences of a political nature are not excluded. The proportion of restruck to regular coins (1:3), as well as the great differences in the weights of the coins (the difference between the lightest and the heaviest is about 3.50 g.) do not contradict the general regular processes in Type 6, established in the above items. Up to 306 B.C. restriking was very intensively carried out.

The hoard from the village of Dogandji (today Sokolitsa near Karlovo) discovered as early as 1912, is of great importance.[48] It also consists of coins of type 6 (17, of which 15 have been preserved). However, this hoard is dated after 301, since two overstruck coins of Lysimachus with trophy were among them, and one on a coin of Cassander with lion. Regular foreign coins are lacking, which leads to the idea that at the turn of the fourth and third century B.C. (and these are the last years in which coins of Type 6 were struck) coins of this type were already sufficient in quantity for the needs of circulation. This supposition can also explain the lesser amount of restruck coins — 1/5 in the Dogandji hoard.

In conclusion we should like to draw attention once more to the most interesting and most puzzling coins of Seuthes III — those with his portrait. Numismatists who had studied them, were almost unanimous in attributing them to around 324-323 B.C., and connected them with the revolt of Seuthes against Alexander the Great and Lysimachus. However, it proved that they were the latest type of Seuthes III, which were struck, according to our attribution, after 295. In our opinion there are serious arguments in favour of the idea that Type 7 was not struck by Seuthes himself, but by his heirs. In Early Hellenistic times it was quite unusual for a dynast to place his own image on his coins. Moreover, Seuthes is depicted as an old man with a tired and heavy look. T. Gerassimov established that the coins of Type 7 had as their prototype a statue portrait of the king.[49] Adding to these facts the simple calculations concerning the eventual age of Seuthes III in about 295, it becomes clear that Type 7 was most probably an original posthumous issue of coins through which the glorious ruler was immortalized and deified, on the one hand, while in addition the new rulers of the kingdom were popularized as his successors.

Regarding the place where Seuthes' coins were struck, we have certain material traces at our disposal which localize it precisely in Seuthopolis. We should, above all, draw attention to a coin of Type 6, which has remained unfinished, with a smooth reverse. In the second place the bronze blank, weighing 1.20 g, found together with a coin of Type 2, should be noted.

Thus the numismatic material from Seuthopolis characterizes the capital of Seuthes III as a centre of definite economic importance. The variety of the coins used in the city is due to its extensive relations, commercial and political, with other centres of the ancient world. The need for the local circulation of coin types of varying denominational value have had an influence here. Bronze coins predominate in Seuthopolis, which is a sign of the appearance of monetary relations in the domestic trade of the region, more exactly in small-scale commercial operations and of a mass character. This special feature of the economic development should, perhaps, direct further research to the more precise establishment of the extent of the new Hellenistic element in the economic, political and cultural development of Thracian society in the period in which Seuthes III and his successors reigned.

In the first years of the city's existence the bronze coins of Philip II and Alexander the Great were exclusively used in Seuthopolis. The development of local minting of coins began under the influence of their monetary types, and this was undoubtedly stimulated by the striving of Seuthes III to rid himself of political dependence on the Macedonian rulers. His coins mark a new stage in the Thracian minting of coins both in types and in the area in which they circulated. The intention of Seuthes' first coins (most probably of Type 3) was chiefly to popularize the rule of the king and in no case to supplement the insufficiency of foreign coins in the circulation of some of the peripheral regions of Seuthes' kingdom. A hoard from the village of Mogilovo, near Nova Zagora, has come down to us, containing 56 bronze coins of Philip II, 47 of Alexander the Great and one of Seuthes III, of Type 3.[50] Owing to a number of reasons of an economic and political character, it became imperative for Seuthes III to improve his minting of coins and to extend its scale. He began to mint coins of larger values in very large quantities, and possibly also of 2 to 3 denominations at the same time. The beginning of the minting of coins by Seuthes III, characterized as its second stage, is attributed to 313-310 B.C. (the appearance of Type 6). It can definitely be asserted that this second stage was not the result of any arbitrary whim of the king's, but was imposed by the development of circulation all over Seuthes' kingdom. The two hoards of coins of Type 6 — one in the capital and the other in the provincial regions of the kingdom — are proof of this. Their content shows that the coins of Seuthes III were increasingly driving out foreign coins from daily circulation and this trend increased. Many of the foreign coins were used as material for the minting of Seuthes' coins which were already extremely popular.

At the turn of the fourth and third century B.C. coins sufficient in quantity to meet the needs of the local market were minted in Seuthopolis. For this reason overstriking was limited in these years. We consider that it is precisely these years which should be held as marking the greatest economic prosperity of the kingdom of Seuthes. The following one or two decades show a narrowing of the inhabited territory around Seuthopolis, a limiting of the distribution of the last type of Seuthes' coins, no hoards of an economic character of which are known. We should look for the end of the kingdom of Seuthes in 280-279 B.C. No coins dated with certainty after 280 have been found in Seuthopolis.

CHAPTER IV

RELIGION

1. Epigraphical Data on Religion

While data on the burial customs of the Thracians are fairly complete,
knowledge of the religion of the Thracians in the pre-Roman period is extremely scanty. There is still no clear idea as to the religious foundation upon
which religious syncretism developed among the Thracians at a later date, in
the age of Roman rule. It is still impossible to give a definite interpretation
of the numerous religious cults among the Thracians of a later period, although there are numerous epigraphic and figural monuments of the Roman
period at our disposal.

That is precisely why the discovery in Seuthopolis of monuments connected
with the religion of the Thracians of the Early Hellenistic age is of particular
interest.51

The last few lines of the great inscription discovered in 1935, namely from
the 27th to the 34th line, are of particular significance for the present subject.
This part of the inscription reads:

τὸν δὲ ὅρκον τοῦτον γραφῆναι
[ε]ἰστήλας λιθίνας καὶ ἀνατεθῆναι
[ἐ]μμὲγ Καβύληι εἰς τὸ Φωσφόριον καὶ
30   εἰς τὴν ἀγορὰν παρὰ τὸμ βωμὸν τὸν
τοῦ Ἀπόλλωνος,ἐν δὲ Σευθοπόλει εἰς τὸ
ἱερὸν τῶν Θεῶν τῶν Μεγάλων καὶ
εἰς τὴν ἀγορὰν ἐν τῶι τοῦ Διονύσου ἱε[ρῶι]
παρὰ τὸν βωμόν.....

The second inscription was discovered in June 1954 in the last days of the
diggings, when the waters of the River Toundja, held back by the dam wall,
were flooding the ruins of the city, which was rapidly sinking to the bottom of
the lake now being formed. This inscription was found at the agora (Figs.
72, 73). It is a granite block-pediment of the following dimensions: length
- 0.88m, breadth - 0.71m and height - 0.36m. There is a hole in its centre
in which an iron wedge had been thrust and had had lead poured over it. A
two-line inscription in Greek had been cut into the lower half of its horizontal
surface; its letters were rather irregular and rather damaged. The height
of the letters was 0.035 - 0.11m. A plaster cast made it possible to decipher
the following text: Ἀμαίστας Μηδίστα
ἱερητεύσας Διονῦσ[ωι]

43

The translation reads: 'Amaistas, son of Medistas, who was a priest of Dionysus'.

The presence of the iron wedge shows that another object had been soundly attached to the block, possibly a relief, probably in connection with the cult of Dionysus.

Moreover, the position of this pediment was not accidental. The great inscription expressly states that the Temple of Dionysus and his altar stood on the city square. And indeed, in the digging done at the agora the ruins of an important building were found, the plan of which it was not possible to establish because of its extremely ruinous state. Not far from it, in the agora itself, the foundations of an altar, rectangular in form, was found, in the agora it the granite block with the inscription of Amaistas. There can hardly be any doubt that all these finds have a connection with the temenos (holy place) of Dionysus' sanctuary, where Amaistas, son of Medistas, served.

Much has been written about the cult of Dionysus among the Thracians. However, data on this cult in the pre-Roman age are few. Herodotus already mentions a sanctuary of Dionysus on the Pangaeus (Koushnitsa). It was in the hands of the Satrae, but its priests belonged to the tribe of the Bessi. Macrobius speaks of a sanctuary of Dionysus in the Rhodopes, which was round in form (a rotonda). Some consider that it is the same one mentioned by Cassius Dio. Lastly we know that Vologeses, leader of the Thracian uprising against the Romans in 13-11 B.C. was a priest of Dionysus.

For the present, the two inscriptions from Seuthopolis are the earliest epigraphic monuments connected with the cult of Dionysus among the Thracians. Moreover, the inscription of Amaistas is extremely important in another respect. It also sheds new light on the priestly institution among the Thracians. Amaistas, son of Medistas, was a Thracian. Both names are Thracian. Actually the name Amaistas is first met with here, but it is a complex name, composed of two elements which are familiar to us from other Thracian names. However, the name Medistas is also very rarely met with. For the present it is known to us only from two Greek inscriptions. In the inscription from Mesambria the name Medistas was borne by one of the forefathers of the Thracian paradynast Sadalla. One of the sons of the Thracian ruler Kersebleptes (359-341) is also called Medistas in the well-known Decree of Delphi.

The interesting thing about the inscription of Amaistas from Seuthopolis is that he is mentioned as a former priest. The priestly institution among the Thracians in the pre-Roman age can be judged from data provided by certain ancient authors, No matter how fragmentary they may be, they are nevertheless particularly valuable. They actually present a different picture of the priestly institution in various tribes, a picture which reflects the different stages of a common development. The different stages in the individual tribes correspond to the different degree of socio-economic development of these tribes. In certain Thracian tribes, for instance, the religious and political functions were not as yet personally separated. The chieftain of the tribe was at the same time a priest.

A far more advanced phase in this respect is to be found among the Getae, where the priestly institution was already personally separated from the ' kingly' one.

The idea of the ' living god' (Dieu vivant), personified in the high priest regardless of whether the kingly power was also combined in him or not, also formed the grounds for the bearing of priestly rank during a lifetime.

The data provided by the inscription of Amaistas are in total contradiction to this tradition. Amaistas was not a priest for his lifetime. When he made his dedication he no longer had the rank of a priest. A new stage in the development of the priestly institution among the Thracians ought probably to be seen in this fact. Among the Odrysae at the end of the 4th century the development of society had gone very far ahead in every respect. Therefore it was possible for changes to set in as regards the priestly institution as well, which had also been influenced by the Hellenic organization of the cult.

The cult of the Cabeiroi existed in Seuthopolis, and they were venerated under the name of Θεοὶ Μεγάλοι, Θεοὶ Σαμοθράικιοι (the Great Gods, the Gods of Samothrace). Their Sanctuary is mentioned in two places in the large inscription. The first part of the inscription informs us that one of the persons mentioned in it, Epimenes, took refuge in this Sanctuary. But, what is still more important, the inscription also mentions that one of the four slabs with the ὅρκος sworn treaty, was placed in this Sanctuary.

The great inscription from Seuthopolis was actually one of the four copies of this treaty.

As was pointed out, the inscription was found in the largest building in Seuthopolis, whose function was easily determined from its brilliance and its particular location in the plan of the city as a palace, the residence of Seuthes III. However, the circumstance that one of the two slabs with the sworn obligation, intended to be exhibited in Seuthopolis, was found precisely in this building, the circumstance that we established the place of the Sanctuary of Dionysus in the agora, where the other plaque should have been, makes it necessary to accept the fact that, according to the data of the inscription, the residence of Seuthes III included in its plan the sanctuary of the Great Gods. In this case we come upon another form in which the idea of the unity of the kingly and the priestly institution continued to exist among the Thracians. Perhaps at this time when, as was apparent, priests who could be changed (the case of Amaistas) had already appeared among the Odrysae, the priestly functions of the ruler had been restricted only to the narrow circle of the cult of the greatest importance, in this case the cult of the Cabeiroi.

We are aware of the great fame and importance which the cult of the Cabeiroi had acquired in the Hellenistic epoch.[52] In this case the Sanctuary on the Island of Samothrace, which had risen to the status of an important religious centre, particularly in the period of Alexander and his successors, the Diadochi, began to play a major role. It had the right of asylum which a number of eminent political personalities, such as Arsinoë (281-280), the former wife of Lysimachus, and others, availed themselves of. The cult of the Cabeiroi spread rapidly all over the Hellenistic world. At many places they were known as the Great Gods (Θεοὶ Μεγάλοι), or the Samothracian gods (Θεοὶ Σαμοθραίκιον). The Thracian lands did not remain untouched in this respect.

However, the monuments of the Thracian epoch known to us so far concern the Greek colonies along the Black Sea coast and the Propontis (the shores of the Sea of Marmara) almost without exception. Of the pre-Roman period there is an inscription from Dionysopolis (48 B.C.); one from Istria - (of the turn of the third and second centuries B.C.); from Sestos, one of about 210-205 B.C. Only in one inscription from Odessos, dated about the year 100 B.C., is a temple of the Great Gods mentioned which was to be found in this city and which was called Samothrakion. It is apparent from these examples that, for the time being the great inscription of Seuthopolis offers us the earliest data on the penetration of the cult of the Great Gods (in any case before the beginning of the third century B.C.) in Thrace in general, that this cult found fertile soil in the Greek colonies on the Thracian coast, and that it had also struck deep roots among the Thracians as early as the Early Hellenistic age. It would appear that the cult of the Great Gods in Seuthopolis penetrated directly from the Island of Samothrace and not, as is supposed of other Greek cults, through the Greek Black Sea colonies.

We mentioned above the great fame of the temple of the Cabeiroi on the Island of Samothrace. Let it not be forgotten that the archaeological finds in Seuthopolis, particularly the amphorae with Thasos stamps, indicate without any doubt whatever the active relations which existed in the Early Hellenistic age between this Thracian centre and the Northern Aegean Islands. The unusual plan of the palace-temple in Seuthopolis, the closest parallels to which are found precisely in the plan of the Herakleion (the sanctuary of Herakles) on the Island of Thasos, favours this supposition.[53]

From the text of the great inscription we learn that besides in Seuthopolis two slabs with the sworn pledge were to be exhibited in the city of Kabyle, and that one was in the Phosphorion and the other at the altar of Apollo, which was in the agora.

The city of Kabyle is well known to us from the literary sources of Greek authors.[54] It is already mentioned by Demosthenes in connection with the campaigns of Philip II in Thrace in 342-341. The site of the city can be considered as having been established with great certainty in the valley of the Middle Toundja, near the town of Yambol at the hill Taoushantepé (Hare's Hill), where ruins of an ancient settlement can be seen.

The new inscription gives us a quite new idea of the character of this city. The Thracian city of Kabyle, which already existed at the turn of the fourth and third century, attained great prosperity. It was one of the principal city centres of Thrace. It had an agora, and important buildings, such as the Φωσφόριον (Phosphorion) already mentioned.

The word Φωσφόριον is rarely met with.[55] It has various meanings: in one inscription from the Island of Mikonos the word Φωσφόριον is used in the sense of πρόσωπον Φωσφόρου i.e. image of the goddess Φώσφορος In Geographi Minores it means Φωσφόρου ἱερόν i.e. Sanctuary of Hecate,

46

situated on the Bosporus near Byzantion. In this sense we find this word also in accounts for the building of the Didymaion. According to B. Haussoullier, a small temple of the goddess Phosphoros, situated somewhere in the _temenos_ of the Temple of Apollo in Didyma, should be understood under Φωσφόριον. An inscription found in the Delphinion of Miletus, assigned to the first half of the first century B.C., informs us about an altar which was dedicated to Phosphoros, under whose name the goddess Hecate was venerated in the Delphinion.

In the inscription from Seuthopolis it is quite clear that the word Φωσφόριον signifies a temple dedicated to a deity, which bore the epithet Φώσφορος. This epithet is, actually, very widespread, being given to various deities: Persephone, Hestia, Hera, Selena, Athene, Hephaestus, Artemis and Hecate, who is identified with the latter goddess. Because of this, the proper name being lacking, it is difficult to define by the epithet alone the cult of which deity a particular monument is dedicated. However, as far as the Temple of Φώσφορος in Kabyle is concerned, it is possible to determine quite certainly which deity was venerated under this epithet. It has to be accepted, above all, that the Phosphorion in Kabyle must have been one of the principal ones in this city, since that was where official acts, such as the sworn pledge of Seuthopolis, were to be exhibited. In this case the coins struck in Kabyle in the Hellenistic age are of assistance. The head of Apollo or the head of Heracles is depicted on their obverse. However, all of them, regardless of their nominal value, have an image of Artemis, depicted as Hecate with one or two long torches, on the reverse.

It is not at all by chance that the figure of Hecate-Artemis should appear on the reverse of all the coins struck in Kabyle known so far, although the goddess is depicted in a different iconographic aspect. It indicates that in this case a certain syncretic cult is in question, whose centre should be sought for precisely in the Φωσφόριον i.e. the Sanctuary of Hecate, identified with Artemis in this case, who here, too, as the afore-mentioned examples show, bore the epithet of Φώσφορος.

Incidentally the cult of Artemis among the Thracians, a cult which was early identifed with that of the Thracian Bendis, is also evidenced by Herodotus.

However, the Seuthopolis inscription, as well as the coins from Kabyle which are dated to the third century B.C., are for the time being the only sources to reveal the cult of Hecate, identified in the concrete case with that of Artemis, a cult widespread among the Thracians at a very early time.

Another special feature of the Kabyle coins should be noted: the picture of Heracles' club beside the image of the goddess, which is most consistently found in all the coins with the exception of a few of the lowest value. This leads to the supposition that certain closer connections had already been extablished at that time between the cult of Hecate-Artemis in Kabyle and the cult of Heracles. It would not be surprising if there had also been a small temple dedicated to the cult of Heracles in the _temenos_ of the Phosphorion. Certain archaeological finds from Thracian burials, such as the images on certain Thracian coins, are quite eloquent proof of the early spread of the cult of Heracles among the Thracians.

47

However, if so far no direct information has come down to us about the cult of Heracles in Kabyle, the inscription found in Seuthopolis expressly gives information on the existence in this city of the cult of Apollo: an altar to this deity, around which official decrees and other state orders were also exhibited, is known to have stood in the agora. Perhaps it is in connection with the great importance of and the fame enjoyed by the veneration of Apollo in Kabyle that most of the coins of this city have an image of this god on their obverse.

The cult of Apollo also penetrated into the interior of Thrace fairly early. A number of archaeological finds from Thracian burials indicate this, as does the inscription from Batkoun, in the interior of Thrace, belonging to the Hellenistic age. The fact that the Temple of Apollo is mentioned in it shows that this inscription must have come from a considerable settlement which was also of a city type.

The newly-discovered inscription of Seuthopolis, as well as the larger part of the other finds from this city, shed quite a new light on the culture of the central regions of Thrace, between Stara Planina (the Balkan Range) and the Rhodopes, and particularly between Stara Planina and the Sredna Gora Mountains.

In the Early Hellenistic age the Thracians of the Valley of the Hebros and the Tonsos had already adopted many elements of the material and spirirtual culture of the Eastern Mediterranean peoples. This fact is reflected in the religious relationships, as well as in the penetration of Greek into the official and state documents of Thracian society. This is most clearly shown in our inscriptions.

Here the question no longer arises of a Hellenization of only the members of the ruling dynasties and their relations, but of the influence of the Eastern Mediterranean culture, which had at that time reached many aspects of the life of a wider circle of Thracian society in the cities.

2. Cult Hearths

A remarkable group of cult monuments found in Seuthopolis also offers interesting data on the Thracian religion.[56] This group consists of about 30 well preserved altars made of clay, of various sizes, from 0.65 to 1.50m, square or rectangular in form. They are made of clay generously mixed with quartz in the form of small low platforms, rising from 10 to 15 cm above the floor. This rough nucleus had a thin layer of fine plaster spread over it on all sides, after which the damp, carefully smoothed surface, was ornamented with various decorative motifs, by imprinting with a cord or special small stamps.

After being baked, the surface of the little platform was much hardened and obtained the strength and smoothness of cement, while the interior, baked to a brick red, remained extremely crumbly.

A hearth was found in each dwelling. In the palace there were two hearths: one, well preserved, was found in the hall which was part of the Sanctuary of the Great Samothracian Gods (Fig. 74), and the second, badly damaged, in the throne room. This is the largest hearth discovered in Seuthopolis, its sides being about 3m long, and corresponding to the large dimensions of the room, 18 x 12 m (Fig. 75).

In most cases the largest central or corner rooms in the dwelling, which had no communication with the neighbouring rooms, but had an entrance only giving onto the portico, were kept for the hearths. They were placed opposite the entrance, in the centre of the room, orientated along the direction of its walls. Some of the hearths had a concave circle in the centre, rather like a phiale, around which the ornamentation was disposed, while others had a smooth surface, and more simple decoration, chiefly consisting of geometrical motifs: squares, rectangles and circles, formed by lines imprinted with a cord. Most often their ornamentation consisted of a square, covering the central zone of the hearth, which was of different dimensions, depending on its size: 30, 50 or 70 cms. In three of the hearths the diagonals were inscribed within the inner square, in another, small elliptical pendants protruded from the angles of the square, and in a third, four small rectangles forming a cross were depicted in the central square. The composition of the large hearth in the palace, which can be quite exactly restored, is most original: four rectangular panels of the same length and breadth are placed around a central square with a side 1.50 m long; they are framed by narrow bands in which a garland of ivy leaves and fruit has been placed. The ornamentation of the hearth found to the South of House No. 12 is most interesting. In its centre there is a small circle with ivy leaves in the middle. Four pairs of zig-zag lines radiate from it, forming a cross, probably thunderbolts (Fig. 76). The whole ornamentation is placed in two frames, the inner one square, the outer one cross-shaped formed from several parallel lines. Three more examples, ornamented with concentric circles inscribed in squares, can be assigned to the group of hearths with smooth surfaces. The following group of hearths have a concave circle in the centre, of varying diameters: 0.20, 0.23, 0.30, 0.35 and 0.50 m, with lengths from 2 to 4 cms. Here, too, as in the first group, hearths are found with very simple ornamentation, consisting only of two or three concentric bands inscribed in the square. However, in most of the hearths the band around the concave circles is full of decorative motifs: garlands or rosettes, of ivy leaves, a wreath of alternating stylized leaves and flowers, of leaves in a triangular form and long stems, joined two by two, and in three hearths along the periphery of the central band there was a wreath of laurel leaves (Fig. 77). Combined with a plant ornament there were the images of three snakes, emerging radially from the centre of the concave circle on one of the hearths (Fig. 78). In this group the ornamentation is placed within two or three square frames composed of several parallel lines, with a variety of forms in the angles.

On two of the hearths, from Houses Nos. 11 and 12, the central ornament is framed by a double set of lines broken up in meanders, between which lines small rosettes, leaves and bunches of grapes have been stamped. The surface of one of the hearths is like a beautiful fabric with the various bands coloured red and blue. Here the spiral appears for the first time as a decorative motif. The ornamentation of these hearths shows the artistic sense of the local craftsmen. In spite of a certain repetition of the motifs, circles, squares and rectangles, a great variety has been achieved in shaping the framework of the ornament by the successful combination of a varied number of lines, and the original way in which they have been broken up.

The repertory of plant motifs which decorated the hearths is well known
from other Early Hellenistic monuments, but the manner of ornamenting them
by stamping with a cord bears traces of the old traditions of the Late Bronze
Age.

The rich ornamentation, which is not only of decorative but also of sym-
bolical significance, the coloured surface of the hearths, and the fact that they
are to be found in the throne room and in the Sanctuary of the Great Gods in
the palace, prove without a doubt that these hearths were not intended for
ordinary, domestic use, but appear as the first evidence of cult monuments
ἐσχάραι of a type unknown until recently in Thrace, and of the beliefs and
customs connected with them. Cult hearths were also recently found at the
excavation of the Thracian city of Kabyle. Their cult character is also proved
by the fact that similar altar-hearths have been found in Thracian tumuli of
the fourth century B.C. As early as 1934, Geza Feher announced the finding
of a clay slab in the centre of a burial, in mound No. 2 at the village of Sveshtari
(formerly Moundjilar), Razgrad District, the purpose of which he was unable
to explain. The slab is considerably smaller and lower than the Seuthopolis
altars. It is a small square platform (0.42 x 0.05m), ornamented with inscribed squares outlined by incised lines.[57]

The discovery in 1973 of new cult hearths in the tumulus necropolis near
the village of Golyam Izvor, Razgrad District, convinces us that altar-hearths
had their place not only in the home, but also in the funeral cult of the
Thracians. Ancient traditions, whose roots are to be found in the Creto-
Mycenaean cult, form the foundation of the Thracian religious beliefs connected
with the altar-hearths. The prototype of these altar-hearths is to be found
as early as the Middle Minoan epoch (turn of the third and second millennium)
of Crete. In the Cretan dwelling the domestic hearth was the central point
and cult place of the house and the altar-hearth and table for gifts, on which
libations were poured and honour was done to the domestic deities, developed
from it.[58] As the 'sacred house' of the Priest-King the Palace also possessed
a cult-hearth on which the ruler in person made libations and offered gifts
to the gods.

The cult hearth in the Palace of Phaestos has an amazing resemblance to
the Thracian altars. It is also made of clay, is rectangular in form with a
central hollow and rich ornamentation along the periphery, applied by stamping.
It is obvious that from the dwelling and the palace the hearth-altar had passed
into the eternal dwelling-place of the dead.

In one of the central chambers of the necropolis at Chrysolakos a round
clay altar was found on the floor with an ovoid hollow in its centre in which
there were traces of fire, probably from the burning of aromatic herbs. The
Thracian altars still more closely resemble the altars of the Late Bronze Age
(the middle of the second millennium) in the palaces of Mycenae, Pylos and
Tyryns, in Continental Greece.[59] Here the altars, made of clay, are situated
in the middle of the megaron and are round with a diameter of 3.70 m in
Mycene, 4m in Pylos and 3.59m in Tyryns. The surfaces of the Mycenaean
altars are ornamented with spiral and other ornaments, some of which are
coloured, while others are stamped with a cord. Their monumental dimensions, rich ornamentation and their place in front of the ruler's throne leave

no doubt that they played an important part in the cult ceremonies performed by the kings. The altar in the throne room in Seuthopolis, which in dimensions (3m) was close to the altars of Mycenae, had the same functions, and upon it the Thracian King, like the Mycenaean rulers, offered up sacrifices. These features, which the altars in Thrace had in common with the Mycenaean cult monuments, closely link them with the traditions of the Creto-Mycenaean cult of the Middle and Late Bronze Age. Together with other monuments in Thrace, the Thracian altar-hearths are a survival of the pre-Hellenic Mediterranean cult of the second millennium B.C., which was revived in Thrace in the fifth to fourth century B.C. and indirectly prove the early contacts of Thrace with the Mycenaean world. Other archaeological monuments also provide evidence of the relations between the Balkan lands and the Aegean regions, and the penetration of cultural influences from the south to the most distant regions of the Peninsula. However, the altar from Wietenberg, near Sighişoara in Romania, very close to the altar in the megaron of Mycenae with which it is contemporaneous, is of particular importance in connection with our subject.

Cult hearths have also been discovered in the Early Scythian settlement at the village of Zhabotin, Cherkassky region (Ukrainian SSR, dated to the turn of the seventh and sixth century B.C.). Here a round altar, ornamented with a band of spirals and meanders, well-known from Creto-Mycenaean ornamentation, is better preserved. Altar-hearths of the seventh to third century B.C. have also been found in fortified settlements of the forest-steppe regions around the Dnieper.[60] Some of them have a concave circle in the middle and are ornamented with concentric bands. The old cultural traditions of the Eastern Mediterranean are undoubtedly reflected in these cult monuments. The influence of these traditions can also be traced in the Western part of the Mediterranean basin where in oppidum La Roque (Southern France) three clay altars have been found in sixth to third century B.C. levels.[61] They also have the form of low tables with an even surface and incised ornamentation of geometric motifs, meanders, triskelions and quadriskelions in which a decorative synthesis of Greek and local motifs is discovered.

Similar hearths have been discovered in other parts of Europe: Czechoslovakia, Poland, the Federal German Republic, Denmark and England, where they are also interpreted as altars which copy a specific element of the Greek house. They date to the late La Tène and Early Roman period.[62]

The extensive spread of this type of altar in various regions of the Mediterranean basin in the period from the seventh to the first century B.C. provides undoubted proof that they appeared on the basis of a common prototype, created in the culture of the Eastern Mediterranean in the Creto-Mycenaean epoch, and preserved in the later Greek culture.

The latest examples of altar-hearths are known to us from the second to first century B.C. In this period they appeared in several settlements of the Getae in Romania, situated in the region around the Danube and Moldavia.[63] The two hearths from Poiana have a simple decoration of squares outlined by double incised lines, while one of the hearths found in the palace of the settlement at Popeşti had a richer and more varied ornamentation. The motifs are very close in style to the ornamentation of the hearths of Seuthopolis, which gives grounds for the supposition that this type of cult-object appeared north of the Danube under the influence of the Southern Thracians; for their part, the Getae influenced the religious beliefs and cult rituals of the Scythian population of the steppe regions around the Dnieper, which is expressed in the introduction of a number of cult articles in the fortified settlement of Zolotaya Balka. An altar-hearth, ornamented with solar symbols, was found in one of the rooms here. Clay fire dogs were found near the hearth in Zolotaya Balka, and the hearths in the late stratum at La Roque; they are interpreted as ritual articles and connected with the cult of fire and the hearth. Clay pediments of the fire dog type were also found in Seuthopolis, but it proved impossible to establish a link between them and the altars.

It is not possible either to establish with certainty to which deities the altars were consecrated. The oldest altars of the Creto-Mycenaean cult are usually connected with a home goddess, protectress of the home hearth and the fire, who developed from the domestic snake and was later personified by the Greek Hestia. It is quite possible that some of the altars in Seuthopolis can also have been dedicated to the goddess protectress of the hearth, whose attributes, the snakes, we found on one hearth.

The image of the thunderbolt could signify veneration of a god, ruler of the heavens, while the presence of garlands of ivy leaves and fruit can be explained by the cult of the productive forces of Nature or of Dionysus, for whose veneration in Seuthopolis there are epigraphic and archaeological data. If the veneration of all these deities can only be guessed at, the material from Seuthopolis offers a possibility of establishing with confidence that the altar-hearths here were closely connected with the cult of the Great Gods of Samothrace, in whose Sanctuary one of the two altars in the palace was found. This discovery gives a new direction to the future research into the cult of the Great Gods of Samothrace, and the rituals connected with it. This gives us the right to draw the following conclusion. If libations were poured and aromatic herbs were burnt on the altars in the private dwellings and offerings were made to the domestic gods, the court altars were connected with the most important official cult of the city, the high priest of which appears to have been the King himself.

3. Burial Customs

The excavation and study of the three large tumuli which belong to the necropolis of Seuthopolis considerably extended our knowledge of Thracian tomb architecture and burial customs. Tumuli Nos. 1 and 2 were erected at a distance of 180 to 200 m north-east of the city in the middle of a low terrace on the left bank of the River Golyama Varovitsa not far from the place where it joins the Toundja. The third tumulus was piled up to the west of them, at about 350 m from the city, on the right bank of the Golyama Varovitsa. Alongside the rich burials in the tumuli, an extensive necropolis of the flat tombs of ordinary inhabitants lay near tumuli Nos. 1 and 2. The burial ritual observed in them is cremation, and the furniture was extremely modest: an urn with the remains of the cremated bones among which a bronze coin and a fibula were often placed.

The burial of a young Thracian woman of noble family was found in Tumulus No. 1.[64] The body was cremated at the base of a small stone mound, 2.80m long, 2m wide and 2.70m high, on which a large mound of earth, 11.50m high with a diameter of 51m, was piled. Precious gifts were found in the tomb amid a thick layer of ashes and the remains of small burnt bones: gold jewellery, bronze and silver vessels, Greek vases. The jewellery consisted of a gold necklace, formed of 36 hollow gold beads, welded together from two halves and made of a very high quality gold – 23 carats. Eighteen of the beads were decorated with a fine filigree wire, forming spiral ornaments. At both ends the necklace ended in two large oblong beads (Fig. 79). Two gold earrings of spirally wound wire, decorated with small lions' heads, were also found (Fig. 80) and parts of a funeral wreath composed of thin gilded bronze sheets and gilded clay balls. Jewellery of this type is known from other rich Thracian burials of the fifth to fourth century B.C. The closest parallels are to be found in the two burials of the beehive tomb at Mezek, which are dated by silver drachms of Alexander the Great of his reign or the period immediately following his reign.[65] Familiar forms of fourth century Greek bronze casting are also represented by the metal vessels found in the burial: a shallow tray, an oinochoe (Fig. 81) and a situla. About 30 bronze situlae have been found so far in Thracian burials in Bulgaria, almost all in men's burials of the end of the fifth up to the third quarter of the fourth century B.C.[66] The situla from Tumulus No. 1 belongs to the type with heart-shaped palmettes at the handles, cast separately from the situla, which are dated to the middle and the third quarter of the fourth century (Fig. 82). As to the centre where these situlae were made, there is a great variety of opinion. According to some the artistic conceptions of Ionian art are clearly reflected in them. According to others Corinth could well be their home. However, some of the bronze situlae found in Thrace may well have come from the bronze-casting centres of Attica or the North Peloponnesus.

The Greek vases found in the burial, an aryballos-shaped lekythos with net-like ornament and a black-glaze lamp are of Attic origin and characteristic of the last quarter of the fourth century. The terracotta, of the Tanagra type, depicting a standing female figure in a chiton and a himation, belongs to the same period (Fig. 83). Moreover, five amphorae with the form characteristic of the Thasos amphorae, had been placed on the periphery of the stone mound. All this allows the burial in Tumulus No. 1 to be dated to the early years of the last quarter of the fourth century B.C. The embankment of the mound also contained a variety of materials – potsherds and bronze coins, chiefly of Philip II and Alexander III. The soil for it was undoubtedly taken from the Thracian settlement which existed here before Seuthopolis was built, and was destroyed at the time of the struggles between the Macedonians and the Thracians.

Tumulus No. 2 is only 20m distant from Tumulus No. 1. It was 8m high and had a diameter of 41-43m. A beehive tomb lying north-south with the entrance on the south side was found in its southern half (Figs. 84, 85). The tomb consists of a stone antechamber, a dromos and a round domed chamber, whose plan it was possible to establish by the contours of the cover of river stones which had been preserved and which had enveloped the body of the tomb on the outside, probably to lighten the heavy pressure of the earth piled up on top of it and also to keep the damp out. The tomb had been destroyed and robbed in Antiquity. Only in the dromos were several vessels found, among which was a Thasos amphora with a stamp. The dromos and the round section of

the tomb were built of baked bricks which had been used after its destruction
to build two one-chamber tombs in the western half of the tumulus - tombs
Nos. 2 and 3. Both tombs lay east-west and were rectangular in plan. They
were built of 10 and 11 rows respectively of trapezoidal bricks and covered
with stone blocks. In tomb No. 2 the bricks were placed horizontally, the
larger convex arc alternating with the smaller concave arc (Fig. 86). In this
way a rectangle was obtained from a pair of bricks and the carrying surface
was not infringed by the trapezoidal form of the bricks. In tomb No. 3 the
bricks were placed longitudinally: four bricks on the long sides of the tombs
and two each on the short sides (Figs. 87, 88, 89). This manner of building
left part of the wide convex side of the brick sticking out like a decorative
tooth. The burials in both tombs showed inhumation. A young girl was buried
in Tomb No. 2, as was extablished by the anthropological study of the skeleton[67] and the nature of the burial gifts left near it: a necklace composed of
hollow gold beads (22 carats), of which 13 were preserved (Fig. 90). Six of the
the beads were smooth and the remaining seven had filigree decoration consisting of a fine gold wire wound around in parallel. The necklace was probably the work of a local goldsmith and was made under the influence of a
Hellenistic model. Two small gold fibulae with bilateral spirals in which the
influence of the La Tène fibulae is strongly felt (Fig. 91), two silver fibulae
of the Thracian type and a small gold medallion with the head of a youth,
worked in repoussé, had also been locally made (Fig. 92). In the other tomb
a boy, no older than 20, had been buried and an iron spear and strigil had
been laid beside him. Part of a linen fabric, probably from the cloak which
covered the buried boy, had been preserved on them. Three clay vessels,
of grey clay, locally made (a ewer, oinochoe and bowl), a Greek black glaze
lamp of Attic origin, a gold earring and burial wreath made of thin bronze
leaves and small clay balls gilded, were also found here (Figs. 93, 94).
Wreaths of this kind were also found in other Thracian burials of the fourth to
third century B.C., and also in the cemeteries of the Black Sea colonies of
Odessos and Apollonia. Five coins were also found in the tomb, four of them
bronze of Seuthes III's Type 7, and the fifth a drachm of Alexander the Great,
minted in Lampsacus, which may be attributed to the posthumous issues minted after the death of the king at the end of the fourth century. On the Eastern
side of the tomb, after the burial ritual had been carried out and the tomb had
been covered with stone blocks, two clay bowls, one covering the other, an
amphora and a pile of 50 astragaloi had been placed, amid which were four
small lead lamellae curved like little tubes.

The custom of placing covered bowls in Thracian burials is evidenced by
a number of other cases. This is the first time, however, we have come
across a pile of astragaloi, a custom known to us only from burials in Greece.
There is no doubt that the burial ritual in Tumulus 2 was Thracian. However,
close contact with the Greeks had expressed itself in the cult of the dead as
well, chiefly in the penetration of Greek artefacts in the burial furniture. These
are the lacrimaria and the alabastron in tomb No. 2, the lamp and strigil in
tomb No. 3, and the funeral wreaths.

In Tumulus No. 3, 6m high, diameter 43m, another brick beehive tomb
was discovered, lying north-South with its entrance on the South side (Fig. 95).

It consists of a _dromos_ and a round chamber. The tomb had been destroyed
and robbed in Antiquity. It was full of earth, stones and pieces of brick.
Only the east wall to a height of 1.60m has been preserved of the _dromos_.
Up to the 15th row of bricks (at a height of 1.20m) the wall is almost vertical.
The following five rows of bricks preserved on the wall overhang one another
by 2cm and the triangular pseudo-vault of the _dromos_ was formed in this way.
The inner dimensions of the _dromos_ are 2m in length and 1m in breadth, while
the round domed chamber has a diameter of 2.70m. The dimensions fully
coincide with those of the beehive tomb in Kazanluk, famed for its murals,
but the stone antechamber is lacking here. The round part was built of trapezoidal bricks. The brick wall has only been preserved on the East side to a
height of 0.70m (nine rows) (Figs. 96, 97, 98). It was established that the
lower part was not cylindrical, but began to grow narrow at the foundations.
The vaulting was accomplished by the consecutive recession of the bands of
bricks proceeding upward. The brick body of the tomb was isolated from the
earth of the mound by a cover of closely placed large river stones. At the
entrance to the tomb this cover was shaped into a wall of ashlars with a fine
face, in the centre of which was the entrance with a framework of well-hewn
stone blocks. South of the tomb facade, in front of its east wing, the fore-
quarters of a horse's skeleton with a bit in its mouth was found. In the
Northern half of the mound, near a sacrificial pit in the earth, the skeleton
of a small animal, probably a dog, was found. Skeletons of dogs are known
from other Thracian tumulus burials. On the edge of the mound 12 _pithoi_
were also found, some of which had stone tiles by way of lids. The architectural type of the tombs, the funeral furniture and the finds in the earth mound
of the three tumuli offer a possibility of establishing a relative chronology of
the burials. The earliest is the burial in Tumulus No. 1, which can be dated
to the early years of the last quarter of the fourth century on the basis of the
clay and metal vessels. The beehive tombs in Tumuli Nos. 2 and 3 must have
been erected soon after each other in the last decades of the fourth century.
They were probably destroyed at the same time. The two rectangular tombs
in Tumulus 2 were the latest, and were built of bricks from the destroyed
beehive tomb, after the year 300 B.C.

The faith of the Thracians in a life after death is reflected in the carefully
built tombs, in the rich gifts placed in them and in the large mounds of earth
piled over them. The vessels, weapons and jewellery placed in them were
to serve the buried person after their death. However, while in the fifth
century and the first half of the fourth century very rich burials were found,
in the second half of the fourth century and in the third century a change set
in in the quantity and the character of the burial gifts. This can hardly have
been due only to the material status of the dead or to an economic impoverish-
ment of Thrace in the Hellenistic epoch. The burial ritual, in which the increasing penetration of Greek traits is felt precisely in this period, undoubtedly played an important part in this.[68] It is also noticeable in the necropolis
of Seuthopolis. Although noble representatives of the Thracian ruling class
were buried in the tumuli the funeral gifts were very modest in comparison
with the rich burials of Douvanliy, Dulboki and other sites in the fifth century
B.C. The complex process of cultural interaction between Thracians and
Hellenes is very clearly reflected in Seuthopolis. The Greek influence in the

burial ritual is expressed in the placing of coins, lamps amphorae, strigils and burial wreaths in the tombs, articles which were not found in the earlier Thracian burials. The Greek influence is also to be felt in the single chamber rectangular tombs, while the beehive tombs are an architectural type evidenced in the fourth and third century B.C. chiefly in Thrace. In Greece no beehive tombs of the same epoch have been found, although the tholos was already known in Mycenaean tomb architecture.[69] The discovery of two beehive tombs in the necropolis of Seuthopolis is an important contribution to the study of the tomb architecture of the Thracians. With them the number of beehive tombs found in Thrace rises to 13.[70] The presence of a dromos and a round beehive domed chamber, the tholos, is a distinctive feature of them. The burial included inhumation and was very often accompanied by the burial of a horse. The importance of the newly discovered beehive tombs in Seuthopolis is also increased by the fact that together with the Kazanluk tomb they are the first burial buildings and architectural monuments of the Early Hellenistic age in Thrace to be built of bricks. The rich variety of forms and dimensions found in Thracian bricks was undoubtedly imposed by the original plan and construction of the beehive tombs. The beehive tombs in Tumuli Nos. 2 and 3 should be connected with the period of the greatest economic and cultural flowering of the capital of Seuthes.

CONCLUSION

The excavations at Seuthopolis revealed new and hitherto unknown pages in the history of the material culture of the Thracians in the Early Hellenistic age. It was found that they too had succeeded in developing their own urban culture which, as a rule, did not fall below the urban culture of the Hellenic world in many respects. Naturally, as in all aspects of the life of the Thracians, in the field of town planning and architecture the strong influence of the architecture of the Hellenic world was noticeable, particularly from the fourth century B.C. on. This was actually to be expected and it would be very remarkable were such an influence lacking, as Thracian society developed on the periphery of the classical world. Situated in the Northern part of the Peninsula, far from the major Southern sea routes, long isolated from the highly developed cultural centres of the Near East and the Aegean world, the Thracians lagged behind the tempo of development of the Hellenes in their own economic and social development in the first half of the first millennium. That is why, when they reached the threshold of the class society, the direct contact then established with the classical world through the Greek colonies of the Thracian shores enabled them to acquaint themselves with the more highly developed forms of Hellenic culture and to adopt those of its elements which corresponded to their new forms of life. Moreover, in most cases these elements were creatively adapted to local conditions.

These phenomena were particularly clearly manifested in the architecture and town planning of Seuthopolis. Thus, for instance, in the plan of Seuthopolis the fundamental principles of town planning in the Greek cities of the classical and Hellenistic period were undoubtedly applied. But at the same time we should seek in vain for the closely packed insulae on the principle of grid construction in the newly created and reconstructed Greek towns, with their building plots initially equal in size, as is the case in Olynthus, for instance. This democratic principle, which corresponded to the structure of Greek society, was lacking in Seuthopolis. Here the insulae were not densely built over, the houses were detached, with considerable space between them, and took up building plots of different sizes, of which the largest was occupied by the palace. Undoubtedly, this was the reflection of a different type of society, one in which the unlimited power of a despot, who was assisted by the members of his dynasty and by the tribal princes, predominated. The situation of the palace quarter in Seuthopolis was most interesting. It looked as if it corresponded to the Acropolis in the Greek city. Actually this was not the acropolis of a Greek polis of the classical period, the religious centre of the city and the common refuge of the citizens in times of danger. This was first and foremost a tyrsis, the ruler's fortified palace, where he lived surrounded by his court. In this respect these elements in the plan of Seuthopolis remind one rather of the traditions of the town-planning system of the Eastern despots.

Seuthopolis was a newly-founded city, built at one time according to a previously established plan, just as Alexander the Great and the Diadochi founded their new cities in the days of Seuthes III: the numerous Alexandrias, Antiocheias, Cassandreias and so on. But Seuthes' city was founded immediately next to his tyrsis, which existed previously, and after being destroyed was rebuilt and included within the boundaries of the city as a special isolated quarter.

The capital of Seuthes III acquired the greatest prosperity and importance in the last decades of the fourth century and the first two decades of the third century. Its peaceful development was, however, interrupted by a hostile attack. The strong Thracian fort was destroyed with the help of wall-breaking machines, the stone balls of which were found scattered along the fortress walls. The city was burnt down and probably taken by storm and robbed. A small part of its inhabitants succeeded in saving themselves and after the danger was over they tried to restore individual buildings. Soon, however, life here came fully to an end for many centuries. Only in the 12th century A.D. did a Bulgarian settlement appear on the ruins of Seuthopolis.

The town-planning of Seuthopolis, its architecture, economics and culture show features typical of a Greek polis. However, Seuthopolis was not a city state of the Greek type, but the principal centre - the capital - of a state with an extensive territory, which stretched south of the Balkan Range, along the upper reaches of the Toundja. The king and his relatives lived in the city, together with eminent representatives of the local tribal aristocracy, who owned spacious estates in the vicinity, and rich merchants and craftsmen of local or Greek origin, who succeeded in acquiring considerable wealth. The common population lived outside the fortress walls in poor huts. The potters' and brickmakers' workshops were also probably situated here. The contrast in the way of life and in the various manners of burial among the inhabitants of Seuthopolis clearly emphasizes the differentiation of class and property in Thracian society which had reached early class relations in the Early Hellenistic age.

Seuthopolis was the most important Odrysaean centre in this period with extensive international commercial relations and highly developed local crafts and an artistic industry. The great economic advance and the political importance of Seuthopolis are reflected in the cultural flowering of the city. The high level of urban culture in the capital of Seuthes III disproves the tendentious information of ancient Greek authors about the low level of culture among the Thracians. Having absorbed many elements of the Hellenistic culture, which it elaborated creatively, Seuthopolis also preserved a number of the particular features characteristic of the original Thracian culture.

NOTES

1. Chr. Danov, <u>Drevna Trakiya</u>, Sofia, 1969.

2. Al. Fol, <u>Trakiya i Balkanité prez rannoelinisticheskata epoha</u>, Sofia, 1975, p. 185 sqq.

3. Swoboda, <u>Seuthes III, RE II A</u>, col. 2022, 2023; Y. Todorov, <u>Trakiiskité tsare</u>, GSOu IFF. XXIX, 1933, p. 64 sqq.

4. Al. Fol, <u>Trakiya i Balkanité prez rannoelinistricheskata epoha</u>, Sofia 1975, p. 107, sqq.

5. Diod. XVII, 62, 4-8 and 63, 1-2; A.S. Shofman, <u>Pervii etap antimakedonskogo dvizheniya perioda vostochnikh pohodov Alexandra Makedonskogo</u>, VDI, 4, 1973, p. 117, et sqq.

6. A.S. Shofman, <u>Pervii etap antimakedonskogo dvizheniya perioda vostochnikh pohodov Alexandra Makedonskogo</u>, VDI, 4, 1973, p, 129 et seqq., P.O. Karishkovskii, <u>Moneti zapadnopontiiskikh dinastov naidenie v Severnom Prichernomorie</u>, SA, No. 4, 1962, p. 54; D.M. Pippidi, <u>I Greci nel Basso Danubio Dall' età arcaica alla conquista romana</u>, Milan, 1971, p. 307, note 115.

7. Diod. XVIII, 14, 2-4.

8. M. Cary, <u>A History of the Greek World, 323 to 146 B.C.</u>, London, 1972, p. 117.

9. P. Cloché, <u>La dislocation d'un Empire</u>, Paris 1959, p. 31.

10. P. Cloché, <u>La dislocation d'un Empire</u>, Paris 1959, p. 160; M. Cary, <u>A History of the Greek World, 323 to 146 B.C.</u>, London 1972, p. 118.

11. Diod. XIX, 73.

12. Swoboda, <u>RE, II A</u>, col. 2022; G. Mihailov, <u>Kum istoriyata na Trakiya prez IV-III v.pre.n. era</u>, IAI, XIX, 1955, p. 153.

13. Al. Fol, <u>Trakiya i Balkanité prez rannoelinisticheskata epoha</u>, Sofia, 1975, p. 199 sqq.

14. M. Čičikova, <u>Seuthopolis</u>, Sofia, 1970 and <u>lit.cit.</u>; Chr. Danoff, <u>Seuthopolis, RE</u>, Supple. Bd, 9, 1962, col. 1371-1378.

15. P.O. Karishkovskii, <u>Moneti zapadnopontiiskich dinastov naidenie v Severnom Prichernomorie</u>, SA, No. 4, 1962, p. 53.

16. G. Mihailov, <u>Inscriptiones Graecae in Bulgaria repertae</u>, III 2, Serdicae 1964, p. 148.

17. D.P. Dimitrov, Gradooustroistvo i arkitektura na trakiiskiya grad Seuthopolis, Arheologiya, II, 1960, vol. 1, p. 3 sqq.; idem, Sevtopol - frakiiskii gorod bliz s. Kiprinka, Kazanlukskogo raiona, SA, 1, 1957, p. 199 sqq.; idem. Seuthopolis, Antiquity XXXV, 1961, p. 91 sqq.

18. R. Martin, L'urbanisme dans la Grèce antique, Paris, 1956, p. 121.

19. D.P. Dimitrov, Za oukrepenité vili i rezidentsii ou trakité v predrimskata epoha, Studia in honorem D. Dechev, Sofia, 1958, p. 696 sqq.; idem. Das Entstehen der thrakischen Stadt und die Eigenart ihrer Stadtebaulichen Gestaltung und Architektur, Atti del settimo congresso internazionale di archeologia classica, Rome 1961, vol. 1, p. 381.

20. D.M. Robinson, Haus, RE VII. Suppl., vol. 254; D.M. Robinson and J.W. Graham, Olynthus VIII, The Hellenic House, Baltimore 1938, p. 141-151; J. Walter Graham, Origins and Interrelations of the Greek House and the Roman House, Phoenix, vol. 20, 1966, p. 10 seqq.; J.E. Jones, A.J. Graham and L.H. Sackett, An Attic Country House below the Cave of Pan at Vari, BSA, 68, 1973, p. 361 sqq.

21. L. Zhivkova, The Kazanluk Tomb, 1975.

22. Th. Wiegand und H. Schrader, Priene, Berlin, 1904, p. 308 sqq.; D.M. Robinson, Excavations at Olynthus, XII, 1946, p. 139; M. Bulard, Peintures murales et mosaïques de Délos, Monuments Piot, XIV, 1908, p. 166 sqq.

23. W.B. Dinsmoor, The architecture of ancient Greece, 1950, p. 297, Fig. 109; Th. Wiegand, Milet vol. I, Heft 9 (A.v. Gerkan und F. Krischen, Thermen und Palästren), Berlin 1928, p. 20, Taf. III sqq.

24. M. Launey, Le sanctuaire et le culte d'Héraclès à Thasos, Etudes Thasiennes, I, Paris, 1944, p. 72, sqq.; pl. XIX; J. Pouilloux Recherches sur l'histoire et les cultes de Thasos, I. Etudes thasiennes, III, 1954, p. 364.

25. M. Chichikova, Trakiiskata grobnitsa ot S. Kaloyanovo, Slivenski okrug, IAI, XXXI, 1969, p. 60 sqq.

26. M. Markov, Prinos kum izouchavane istoriyata na bozainitsité v Bulgaria (materiali ot Seuthopolis), Izvestiya na Zoologicheskiya Institut, VII, 1958, p. 143, sqq.

27. M. Čičikova, Développement de la céramique thrace à l'époque classique et hellénistique, AA Phil., Studia archaeologica, Serdicae, 1963, p. 35 sqq.

28. M. Čičikova, Développement de la céramique thrace à l'époque classique et hellénistique, AA Phil., Studia archaeologica, Serdicae, 1963, p. 40 sqq.; idem. Seuthopolis, Sofia, 1970, 60-70.

29. M. Čičikova, Les timbres sur pithoi de Seuthopolis, BCH LXXXII-1958-II, p. 466 sqq.

30. M. Chichikova, Pechati s izobrazhenie na nakiti vurhou pitosi ot Seuthopolis, Studia in honorem D. Dechev, Sofia, 1958, p. 475-487.

31. M.N. Tod, The Greek Numeral Notations, BSA, XVIII, 1911-1912, p. 100 sqq.; idem, Further Notes on the Greek Acrophonic Numerals, BSA, XXVIII, 1926-1927, p. 141.

32. M. Lang, Numerical Notations on Greek Vases, Hesperia, XXV, p. 15 sqq., No. 1-61

33. M. Chichikova, Poyava i oupotreba na touhlata kato stroitelen material ou trakité v kraja na IV i nachaloto na III v pr.n.era. IAI, XXI, 1957, p. 129-152.

34. K. Lehmann, Samothrace: Third Preliminary Report, Hesperia, XIX, No. 1, 1950, p. 14; Peter Robert Franke, Zu einigen Ziegelstempeln aus Epirus Die Antiken Münzen von Epirus. Wiesbaden 1961, p. 312 sqq.

35. D. Robinson, Excavations at Olynthus, Paris VIII, p. 223 sqq.

36. L. Ognenova-Marinova, Notes Sur la toreutique antique en Thrace, Thracia, III, Sofia, 1974, p. 192, Fig. 9-13.

37. A. Alexieva, Amforni pechati ot Koprinka, GNAMPl, II, 1950, p. 185-190; A. Balkanska, Die Handelbeziehungen von Seuthopolis, AAPhil, Studia Archaeologica, Serdicae, 1963, p. 49-59.

38. M. Chichikova, Grutskata keramika ot Seuthopolis, Archeologiya, VII, 1965, vol. 2, p. 34-42.

39. Lilly Ghali-Kahil, La céramique grecque, Etudes thasiennes, VII, Paris, 1960, p. 128 sqq. D. Robinson, Excavations at Olynthus, XIII, p. 274, sqq.

40. T. Ivanov, Antichna keramika ot nekropola na Apoloniya, in Apoloniya, Sofia, 1963, p. 196 sqq., No. 474-478.

41. H.A. Thompson, Two Centuries of Hellenistic Pottery, Hesperia, III, 1934, p. 311 sqq.

42. E.I. Levi, Privoznaya grecheskaya keramika iz razkopok Olvii v 1935 i 1936 g., Olvia I, Kiev 1940, p. 105, sqq.; T.N. Knipovich, Houdozhestvennaya keramika v gorodakh Severnago Prichernomoriya, AGSP, 1955, p. 356, sqq.

43. R.H. Howland, Greek Lamps and Their Survivals, The Athenian Agora, IV, 1958, p. 67 sqq.

44. T.N. Knopovich, K voprossou o torgovih snosheniah antichnih kolonii severnogo Prichernomoriya v epohu elinizma, SA, XI, p. 271 seqq.; J.B. Brashinskii, Afini i Severnoe Prichernomorie v VI-II vv. do n.e., Moskva, 1963, p. 153, sqq.

45. O. Iliescu, Trois monnaies de Seuthes III, Thraco-Dacica, Bucarest, 1976, p. 168, note 27.

46. D.P. Dimitrov, Bronzovi moneti na dinasta Adei ot razkopkite v Seuthopolis, Arheologiya, XIV, 1972, vol. 3, p. 65 sqq.

47. For the chronology of Cassander's coins see Γ.Π.Οίκονόμου, Νομίσματα τοῦ βασιλέως Κασσάνδρου,'Αρχαιολογικόν Δελτίον, 1918, p. 1-29, pl. 1 and the last study of Ch. Ehrhardt, The Coins of Cassander, Journal of Numismatic Fine arts, Vol. 2, 1973, No. 2, p. 26 sqq.

48. Three overstruck coins from the hoard were published by N. Moushmov, Prepechatani antichni moneti, IAI, II 1923/24, p. 174 sqq.; Y. Youroukova, Coins of the Ancient Thracians, B.A.R. Supplementary Series, 4, Oxford 1976, No. 75-83, published 13 coins of the same hoard without mentioning that they came from a collective hoard.

49. T. Gerassimov, Portret na Seuthes III (323-311 g.pr.n.e.) vurhou moneti, IAI, XIX, 1955, p. 123 sqq.

50. T. Gerassimov, Monetni sukrovishta, namereni v Bulgaria prez 1966, IAI, XXX, 1967, p. 188.

51. D.P. Dimitrov, Neuentdeckte epigraphische Denkmäler über die Religion der Thraker in der frühhellenistischen Epoche, Hommages à Waldemar Deonna, Collection Latomus, XXVIII, 1957, p. 181 sqq.; idem, Kum vuprossa za religiyata na trakite ot rannoelinisticheskata epoha, Istoricheski pregled, XVII, 1957, No. 2, p. 65, sqq.

52. B. Hemberg, Die Kabiren, Uppsala, 1950.

53. Etudes Thasiennes, I, 1944, p. 72 sqq.; Etudes Thasienn..s III, 1954, p. 364.

54. Oberhummer, RE, X, 1455.

55. B. Haussoullier, Inscriptions de Didymes, Revue de Philologie, XLIX, 1925, p. 19 sqq.

56. M. Chichikova, Zhertveniki ellinisticheskoi epohi v Thrakii, Studia Thracica, 1, Sofia, 1975, p. 180 sqq.

57. G. Feher, Mogilni nahodki ot Moumdjilar, IAI, VIII, 1934, p. 110 sqq.

58. P. Demargue, Culte funéraire et foyer domestique dans la Crète minoenne, BCH LVI, 1932, p. 76.

59. M.R. Nilsson, The Minoan-Mycenaean Religion and Its Survival in Greek Religion, London, 1927, p. 85, 105; G.E. Mylonas, Ancient Mycenae, London, 1957, p. 54 sqq.

60. E.F. Pokrovskaya, Zhertvennik ranneskifskogo vremeni ou s. Zhabotin. Kratkie soobshteniya, Kiev, No. 12, 1962, p. 73, sqq; M.I. Vyazmitina, Zolota Balka, Kiev, 1962, p. 213, sqq.

61. P.L. Larderet, L'oppidum préromain de la Roque, commune de Fabrègues (Hérault), Gallia, XV, 1957, p. 25 sqq.

62. T. Makiewicz, Oltarze i 'paeniska' ornamentowane z epoki zelaza w Europie, Przeglad Archeologiczny, vol. 24, 1976, p. 103 sqq.

63. Şantierul Poiana, SCIV, III, 1952, p. 194, Fig. 3; R. Vulpe, Şantierul arheologic Popeşti, MCA VI, 1959, p. 308 sqq.

64. K. Zhouglev, Razkopki i proouchvaniya na Mogila No. 1 - Koprinka, GSOu IFF XLVII, 1952, 12, p. 217 sqq.

65. B. Filov, Koupolnité grobnitsi pri Mezek, IAI XI, 1937, p. 75 sqq.

66. M. Chichikova, Trakiiska grobnitsa ot s. Kaloyanovo, Slivenski okrug, IAI, XXI, 1969, p. 68 sqq.

67. P. Boev, Trakiiski antropologicheski materiali ot Seuthopolis, Archeologiya, II, 1960, No. 2, p. 52 sqq.

68. M. Čičikova, Nouvelles fouilles et recherches des nécropoles thraces des Ve-IIIe ss. av.n. ère en Bulgarie, Actes du Ier Congrès International des Etudes balkaniques et sud-est Européennes, II, Sofia, 1969, p. 371 sqq.

69. L. Ognenova, Survivances de la civilisation méditerranéenne de IIe millenaire en Thrace, vers la seconde moitié du Ier millenaire. AAPhil, Studia archaeologica, Serdicae, 1963, p. 27, sqq.

70. V. Mikov, Proizhodat na koupolnite grobnitsi v Trakia, IAI, XIX, 1955, p. 15, sqq.

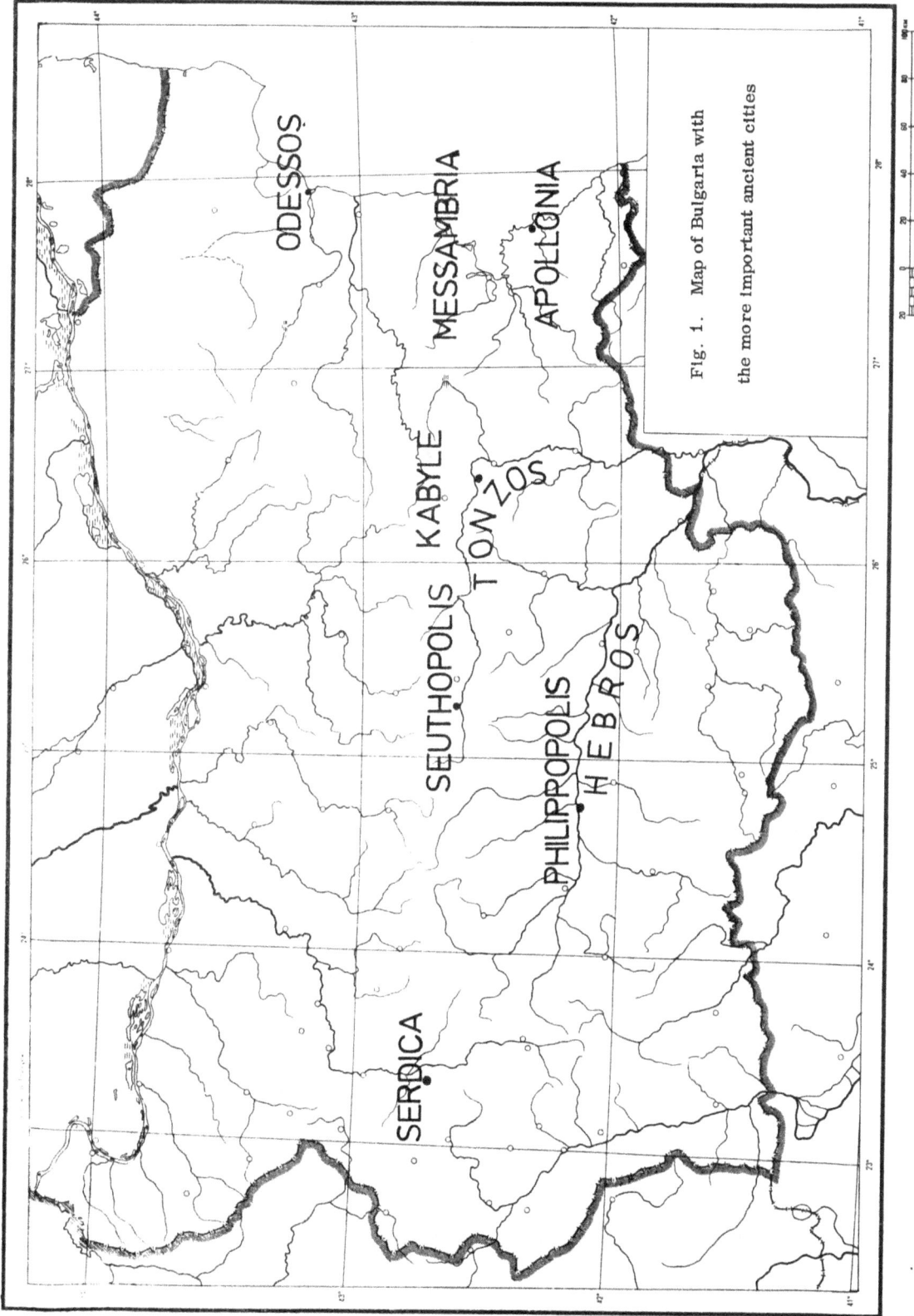

ODESSOS

MESSAMBRIA

APOLLONIA

KABYLE

TONZOS

SEUTHOPOLIS

PHILIPPOPOLIS

HEBROS

SERDICA

Fig. 1. Map of Bulgaria with

the more important ancient cities

Fig. 2. View of Seuthopolis from the South

Fig. 4. Aerial view of the city from the South

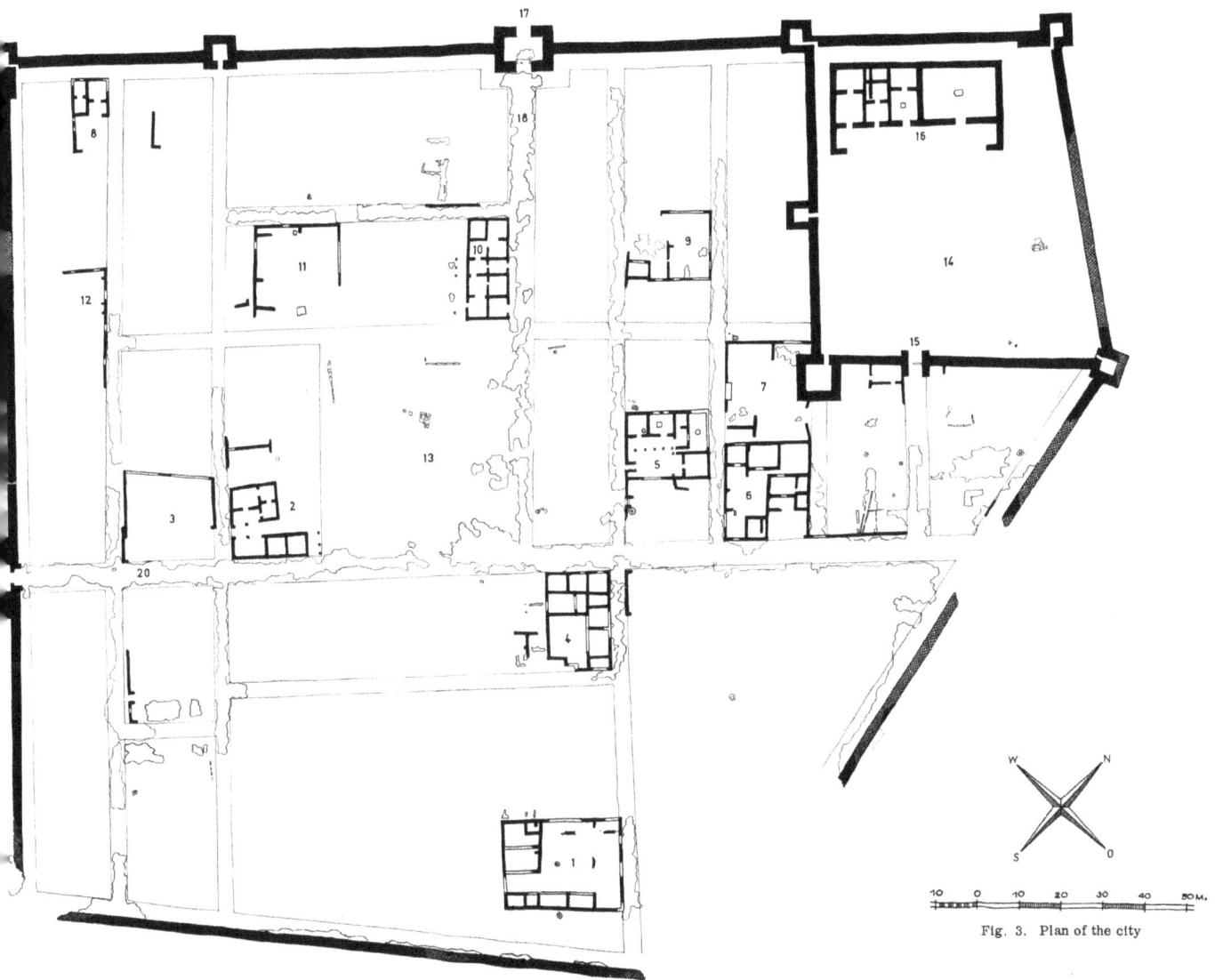

Fig. 3. Plan of the city

Please note that a full-size version of this figure is available to download from
www.barpublishing.com/additional-downloads.html
The original foldout has been reduced in size to match the A4 format of this book, the
image is therefore not as clear as the original foldout. Please refer to the original
foldout via the download for the original content.

Please also be aware that the image might be cut off or not complete in the printed book.

Fig. 5.   Aerial view of the city from the North

Fig. 6.   View of the agora with the altar of Dionysus

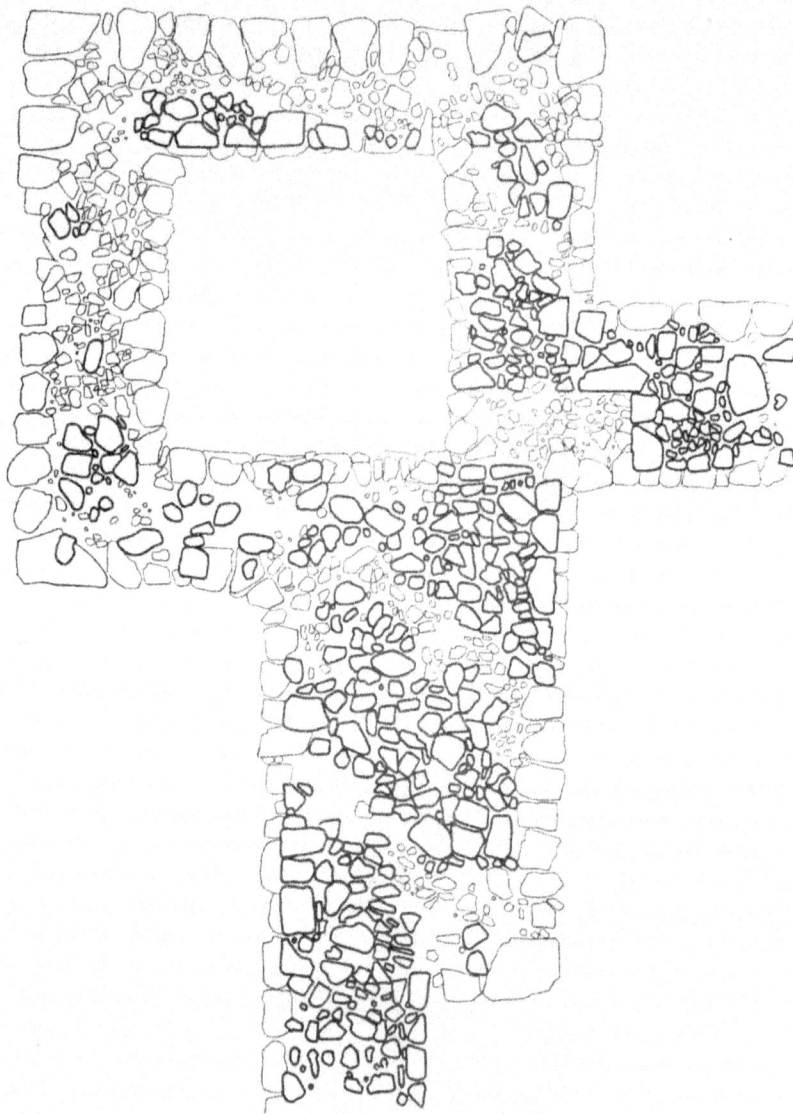

Fig. 8. The Western Corner Tower, plan

Fig. 7. The Western Corner Tower, aerial view

Fig. 9. The North-western Intermediary Tower, seen from the North

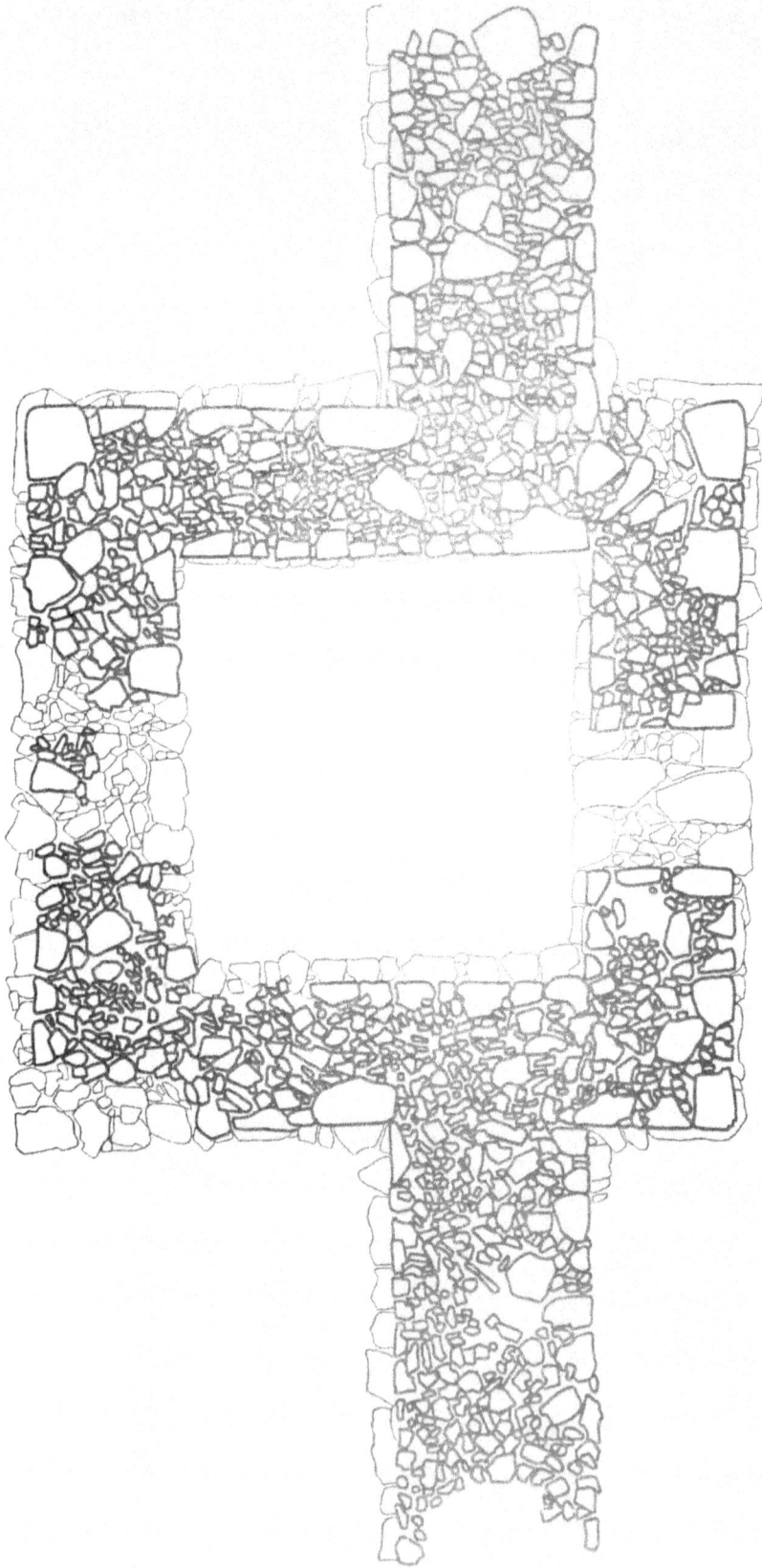

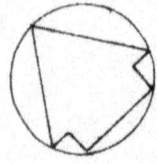

Fig. 10.   The North-western Intermediary Tower, plan

Fig. 11. The South-western wall when it was discovered

Fig. 12. The South-western wall with the Gate, seen from the South

Fig. 13. The South-western Gate, seen from the South-west

a

b   Fig. 15. House No. 5, a. viewed from the West, b. viewed from the
North-west

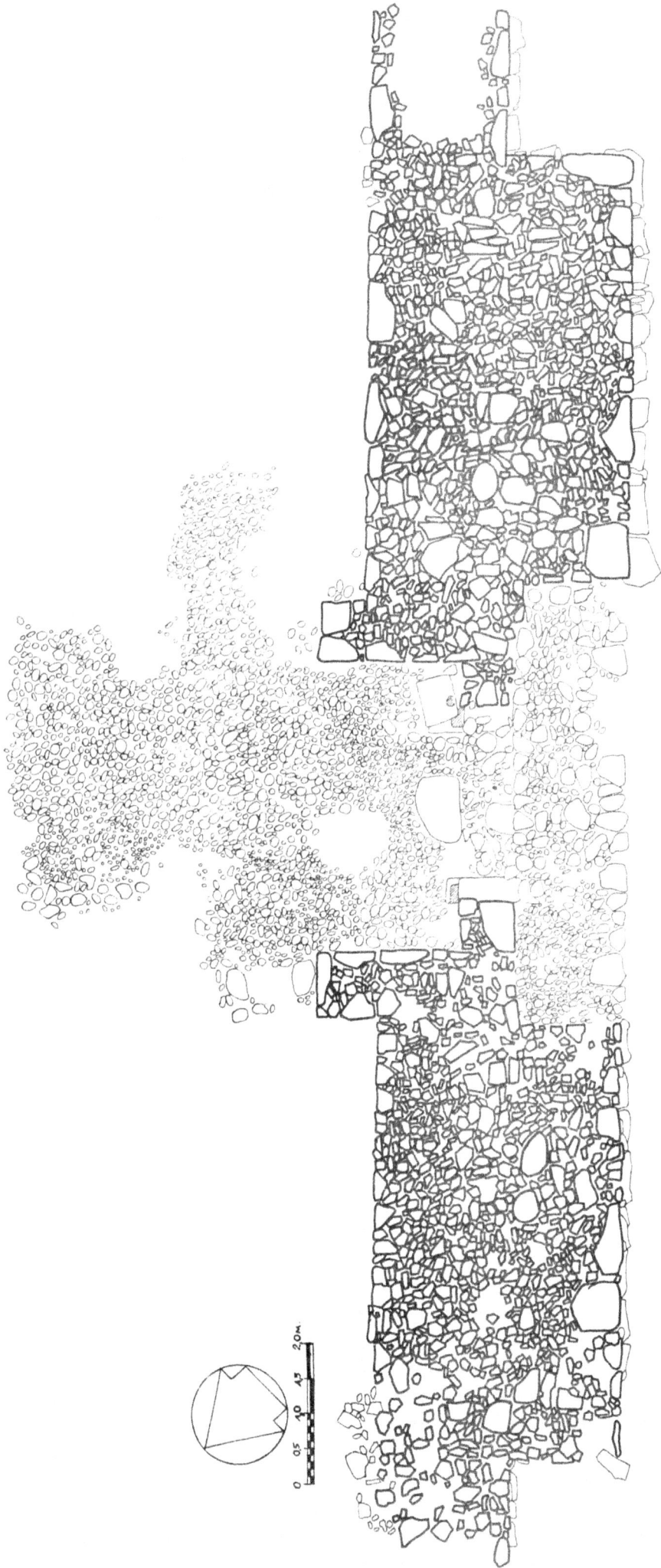

Fig. 14. The South-western Gate, plan

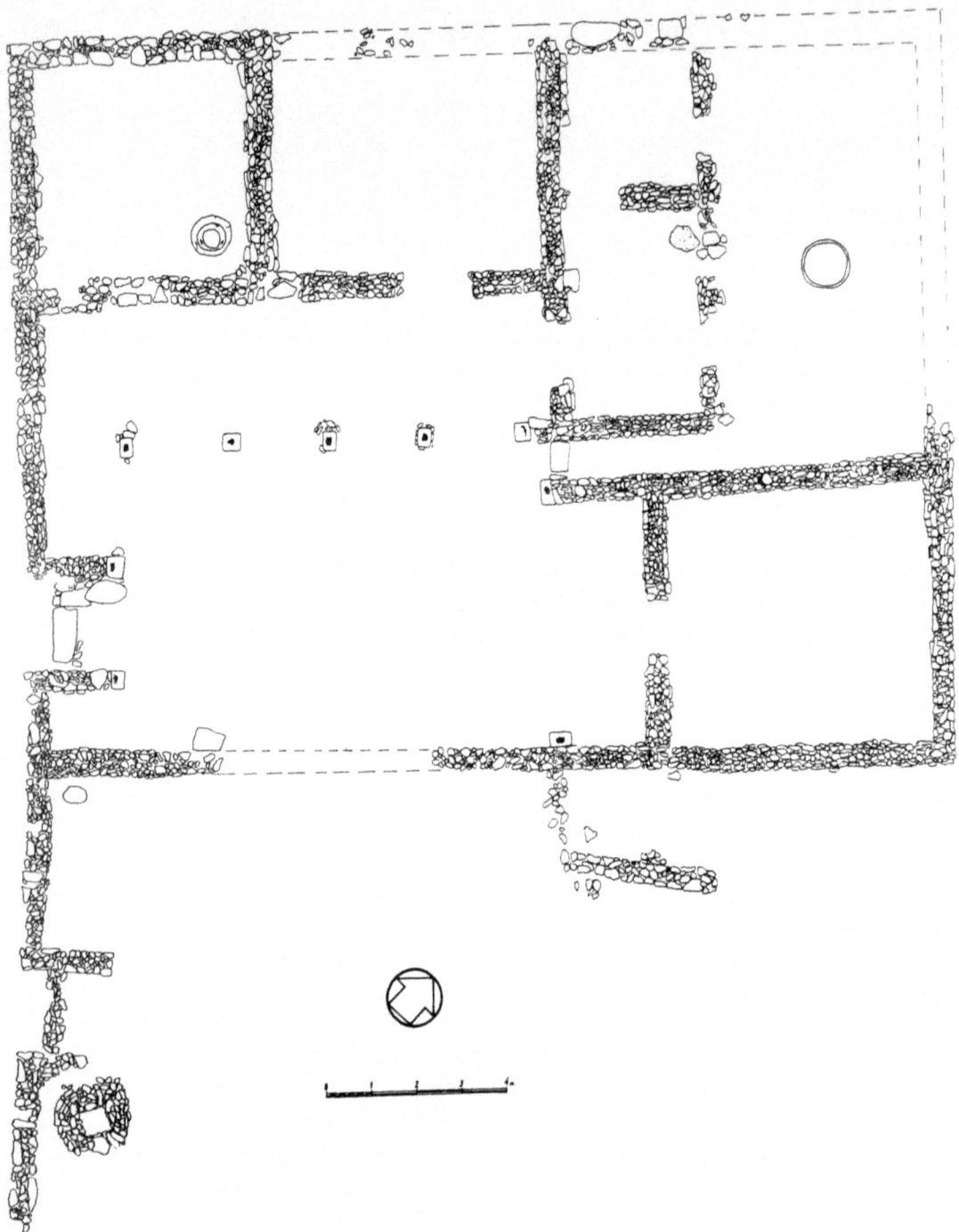

Fig. 17. House No. 5, plan

Fig. 18.   House No. 1, plan

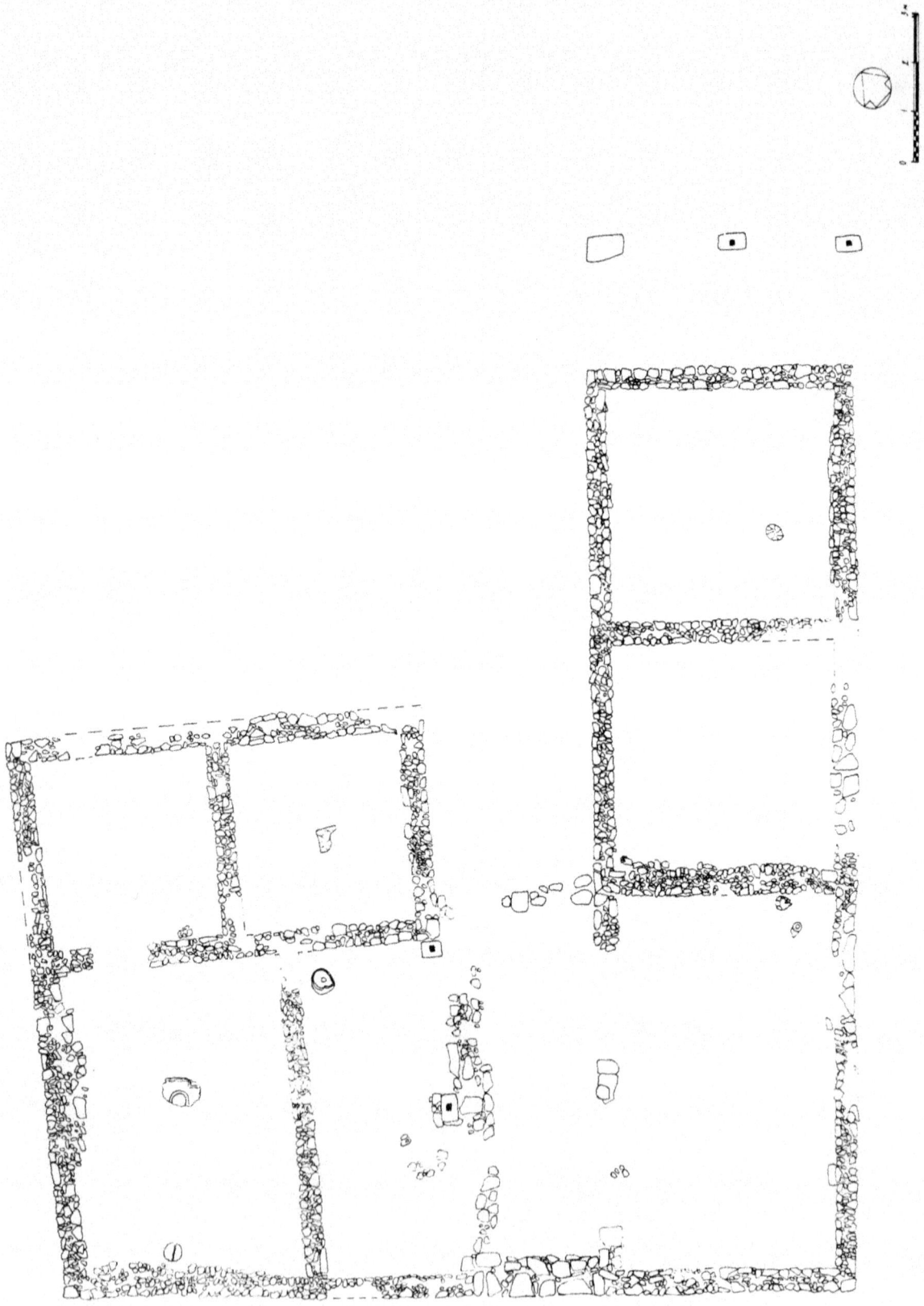

Fig. 20.   House No. 2, plan

Fig. 16. House No. 5, store-room with a pithos

Fig. 19. House No. 2, the North-western part

Fig. 21. House No. 6, viewed from the South-east

a

b   Fig. 22.   Building No. 10, a.   viewed from the West, b.   viewed from the North-west

Fig. 24.   Altar-hearth

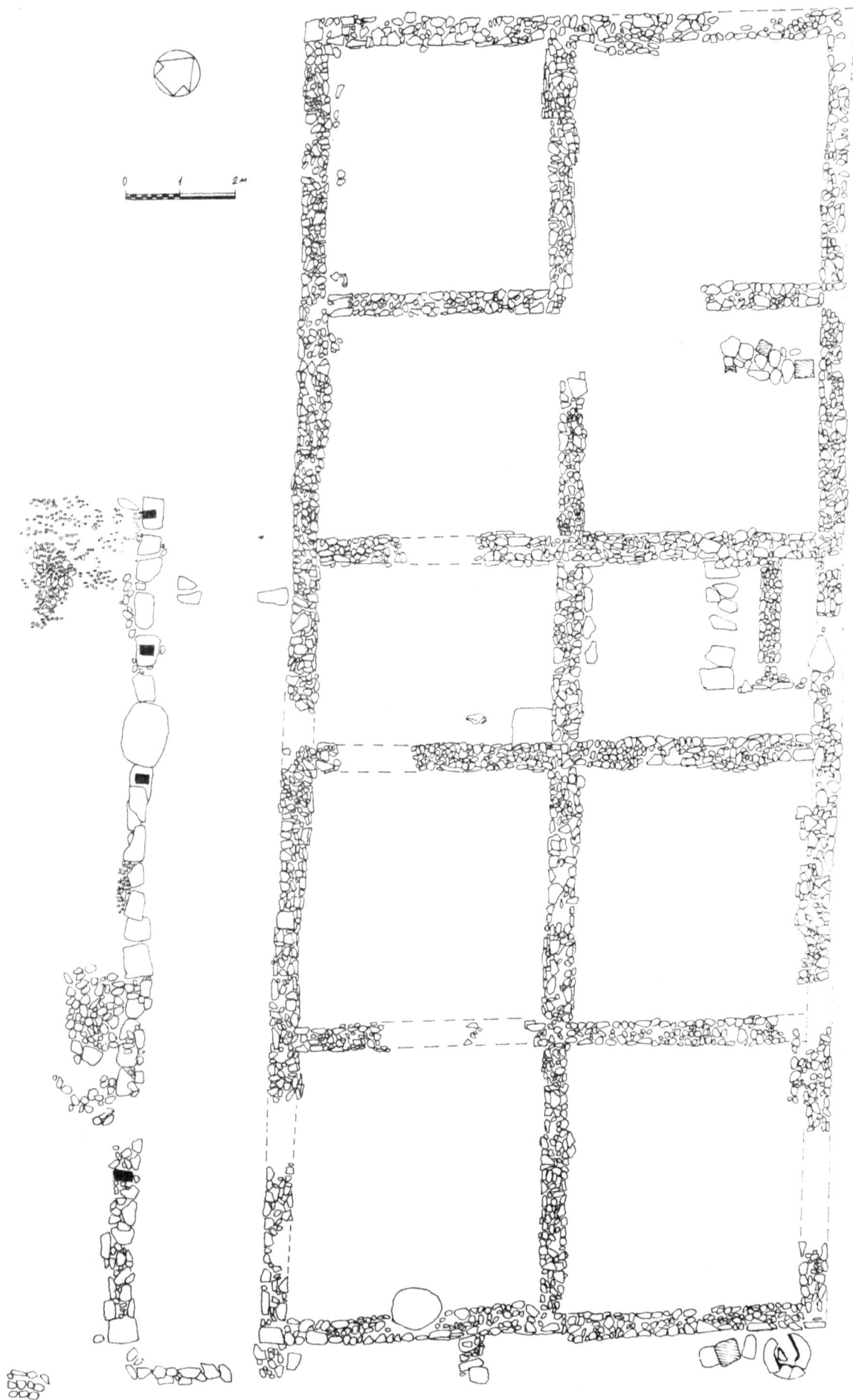

Fig. 23. Building No. 10, plan

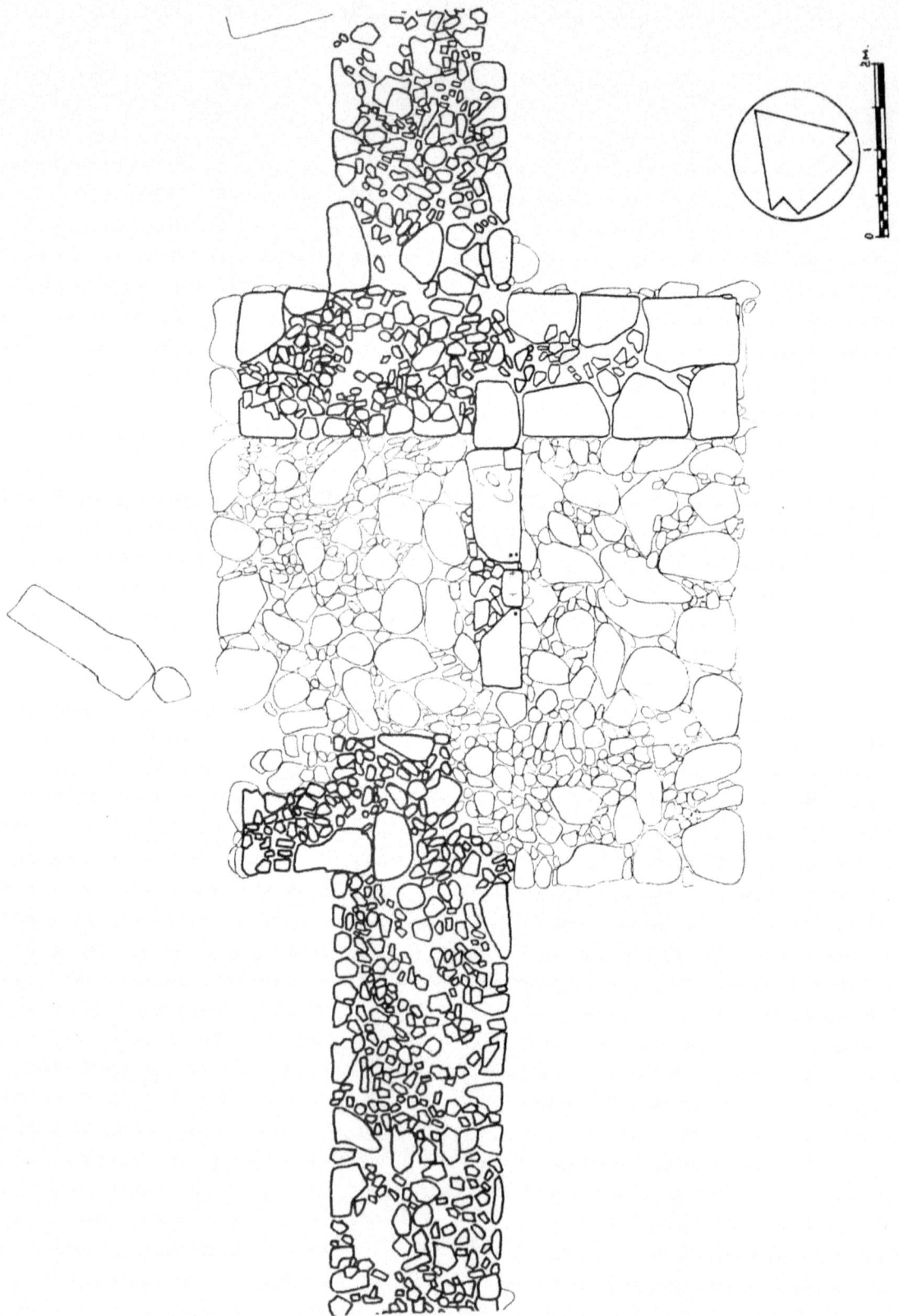

Fig. 26. Entrance to the citadel, plan

Fig. 25. Entrance to the citadel

Fig. 27. Lower drum of a granite column in the Doric style

Fig. 29. The Palace, viewed from the West

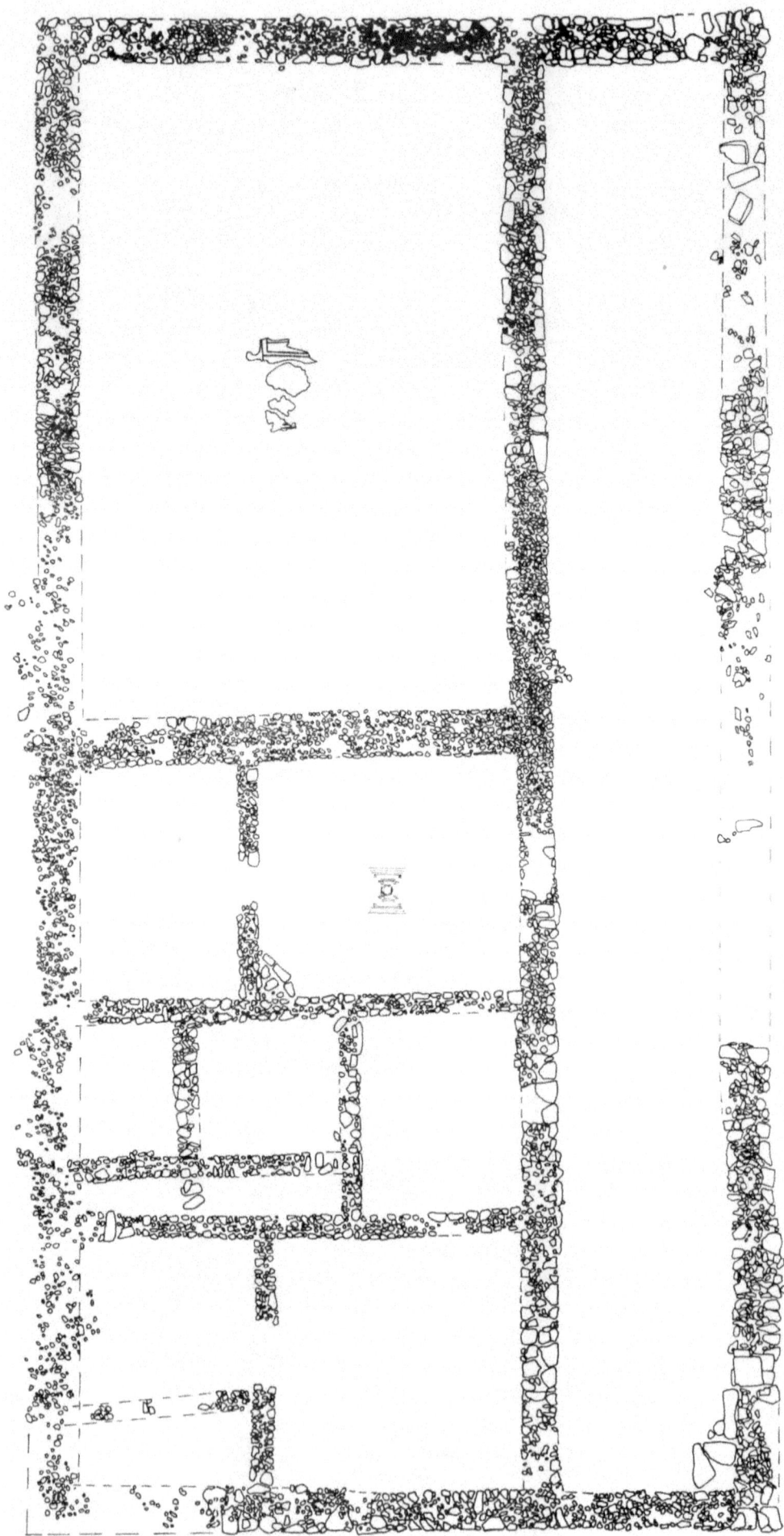

Fig. 28 The Palace plan

Fig. 30. The Palace: the throne room, viewed from the West

Fig. 31. The Palace: the Sanctuary of the Great Samothracian Deities

Fig. 32. The altar-hearth in the Sanctuary

Fig. 34. Brick-lined well

Fig. 33. Antefixes from the Palace

Fig. 35. Querns

Fig. 36. Iron ploughshare

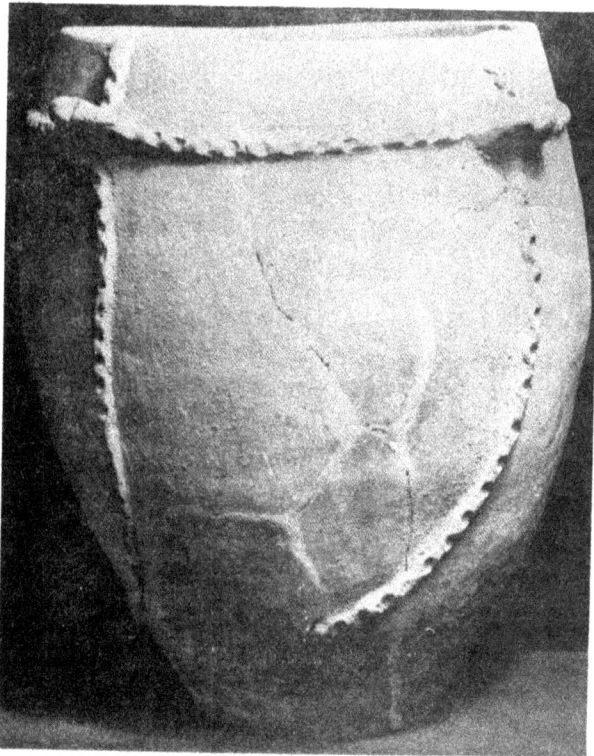

Fig. 37. Hand-made clay vessel

Fig. 38. Hand-made clay vessel

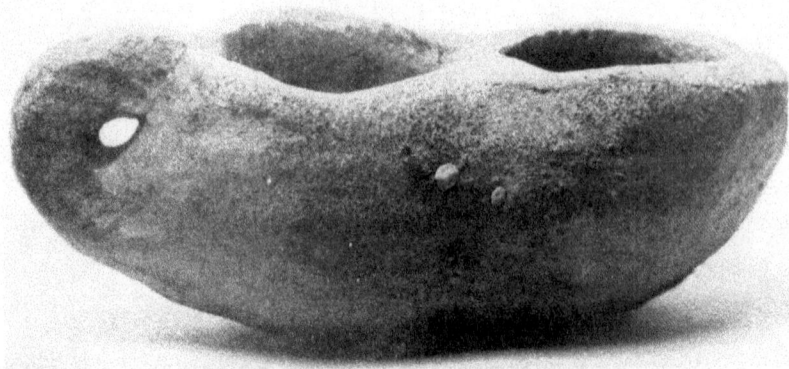

Fig. 39. Hand-made small double vessel

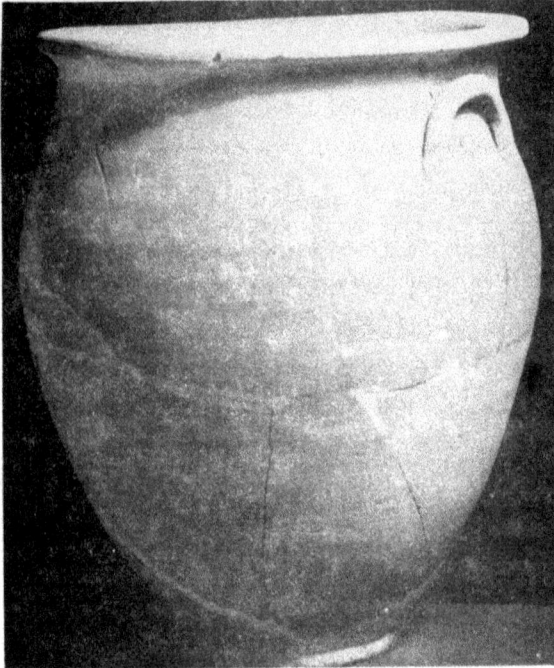

Fig. 40. Krater-shaped clay vessel, wheel-made

Fig. 41. Grey pitcher, wheel-made

Fig. 42. Grey oinochoe

Fig. 43. Grey Kantharos

Fig. 44. Grey bowl

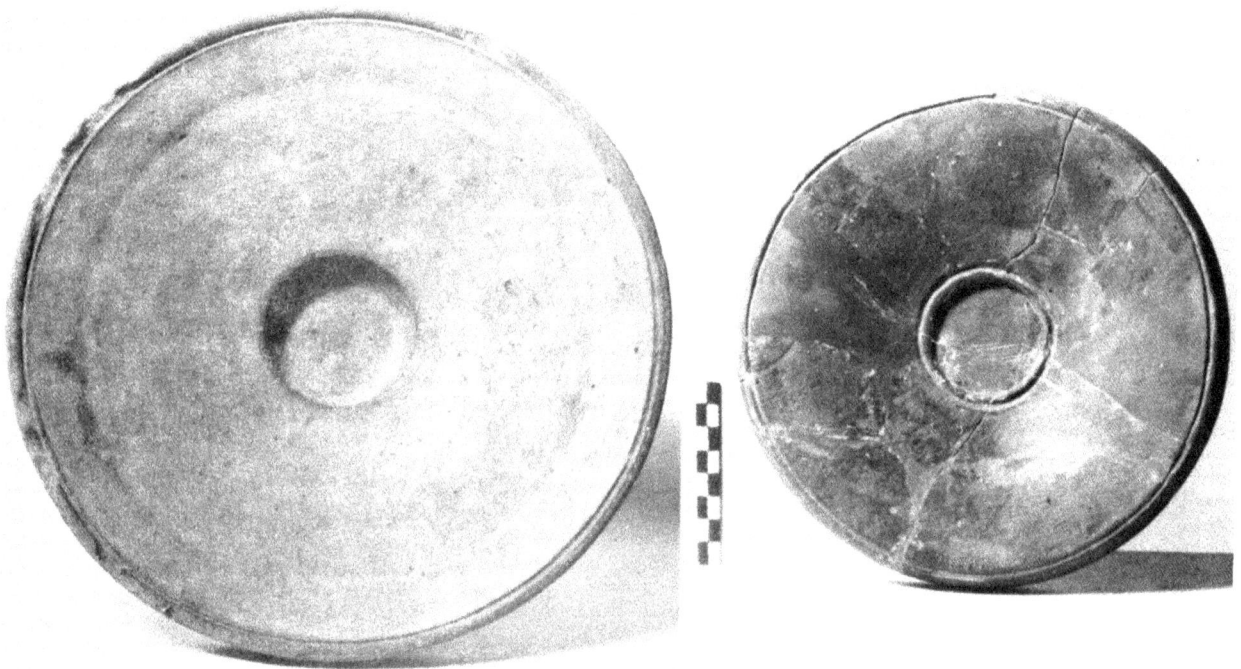

Fig. 45. Fish-plates

Fig. 46. Red-clay bowl

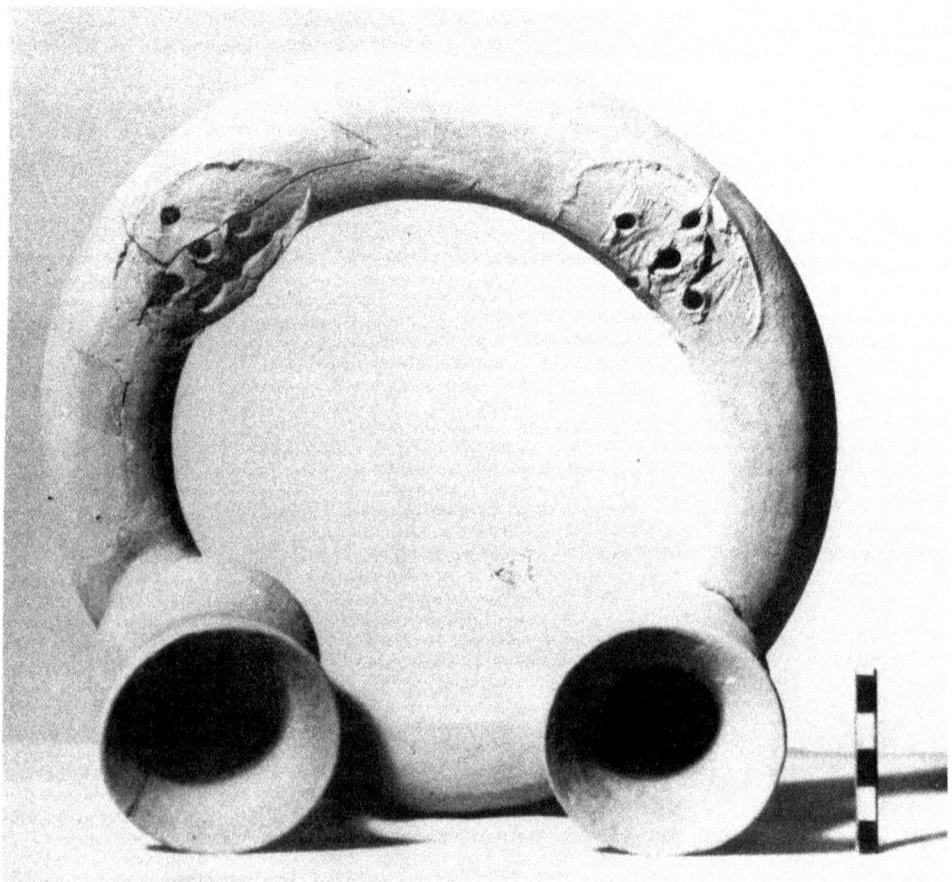

Fig. 47. <u>Kernos</u>

Fig. 48.   Lamp in the shape of a Negro's head

Fig. 49   Pithoi

Fig. 50. Stamps on the mouths of pithoi

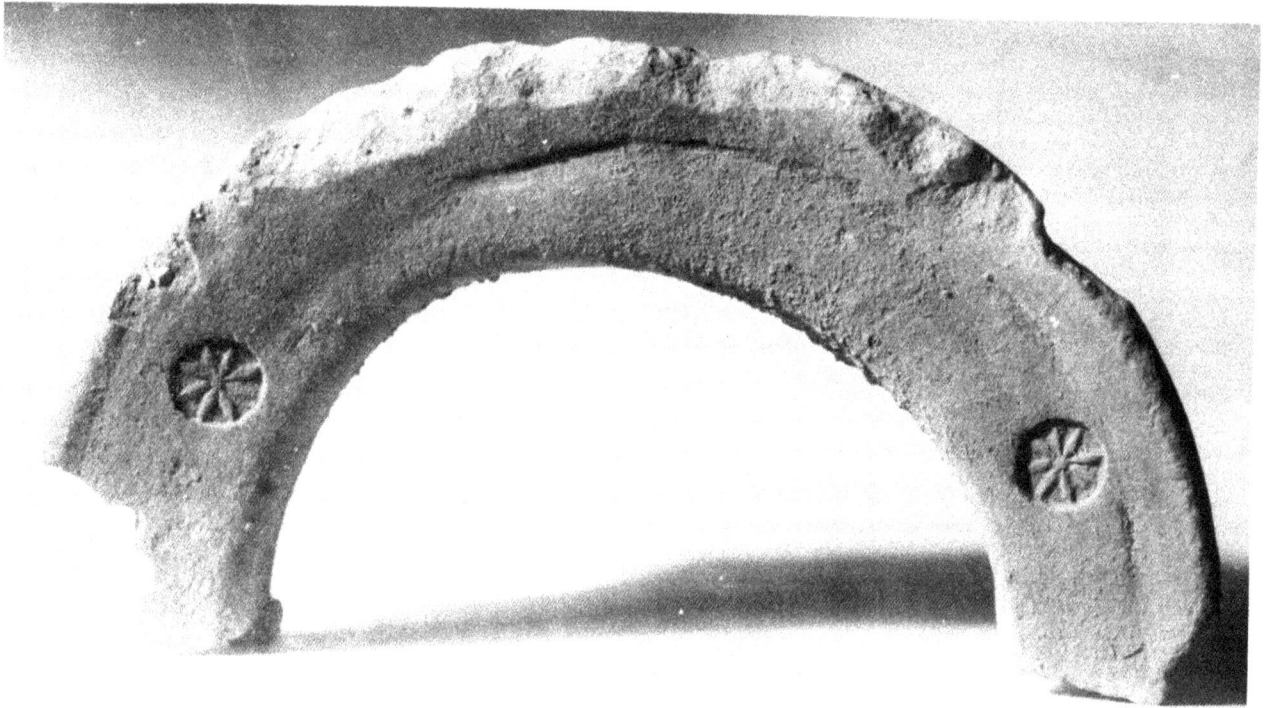

Fig. 51.   Stamps on the mouths of <u>pithoi</u>

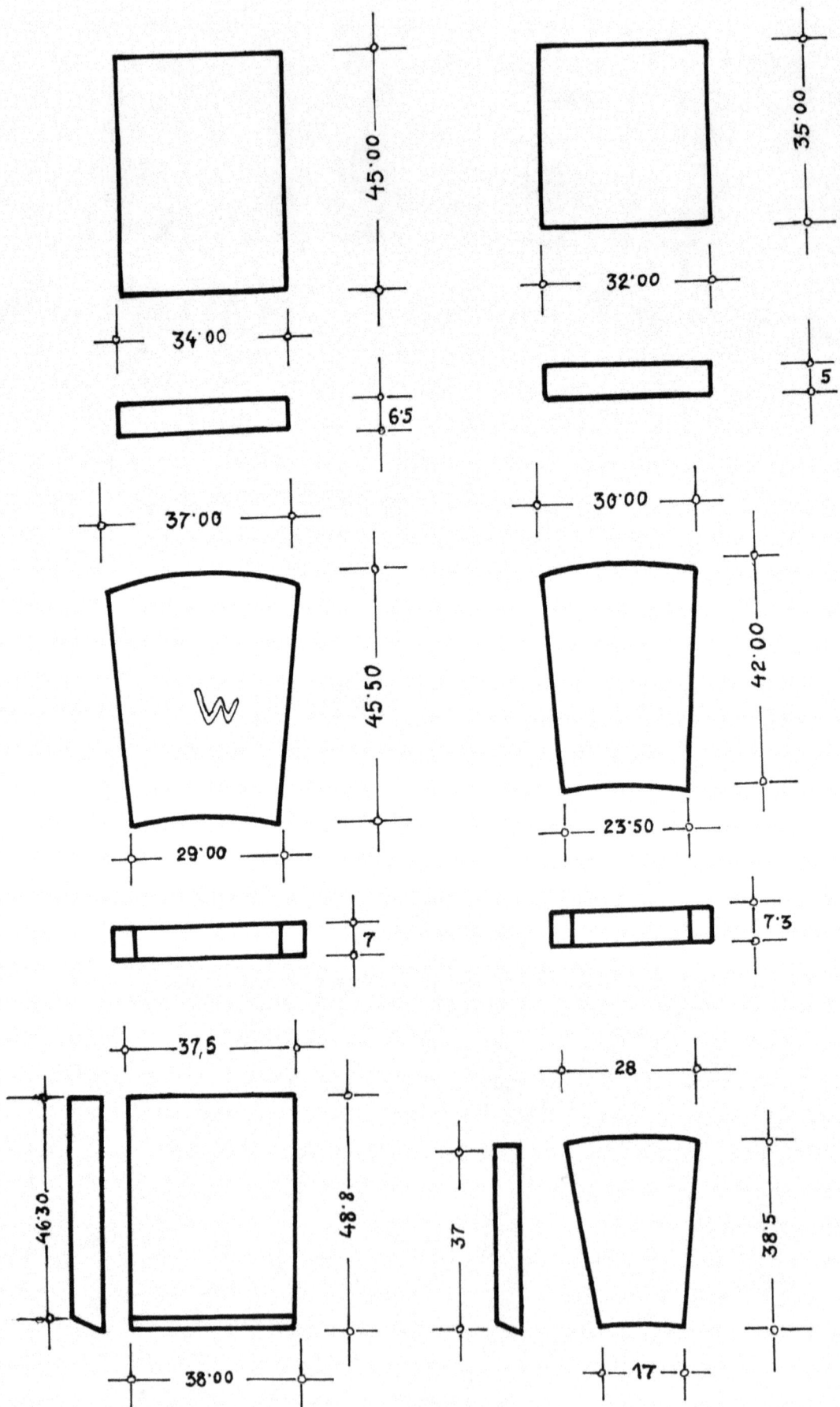

Fig. 52. Rectangular and trapezoid bricks

Fig. 53. Bricks with various signs

Fig. 54. Bricks from a well

Fig. 55. Iron knife and bronze arrow-tips

Fig. 56. Bronze fibulae of the Thracian type

Fig. 57. Snake made of lead

Fig. 58. Stamp on an amphora from Thasos with the emblem of a Negro's head

Fig. 59. Black-glaze kantharos

Fig. 60. Fragments of kantharoi with decoration

Fig. 61. Graffiti on Greek vases

Fig. 62.   Black-glaze lamps

Fig. 63.   Marble relief of a man's head

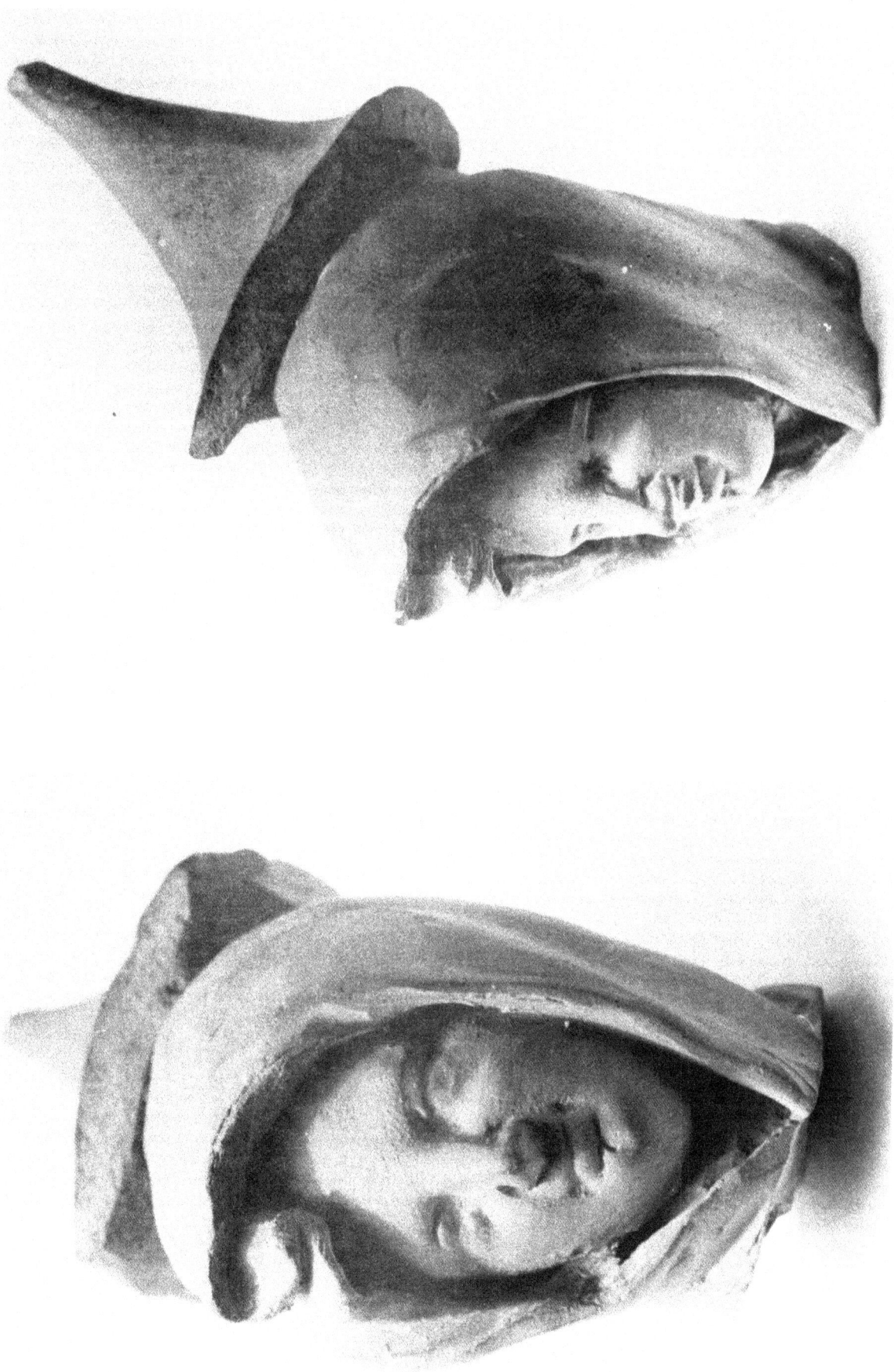

Fig. 64. Woman's head, terracotta (Tanagra type)

Fig. 65. Man's head, architectural terracotta

a

b

Fig. 66. Tetradrachms - a. minted by Lysimachus (magnified)
b. of Alexander the Great (magnified)

a

b

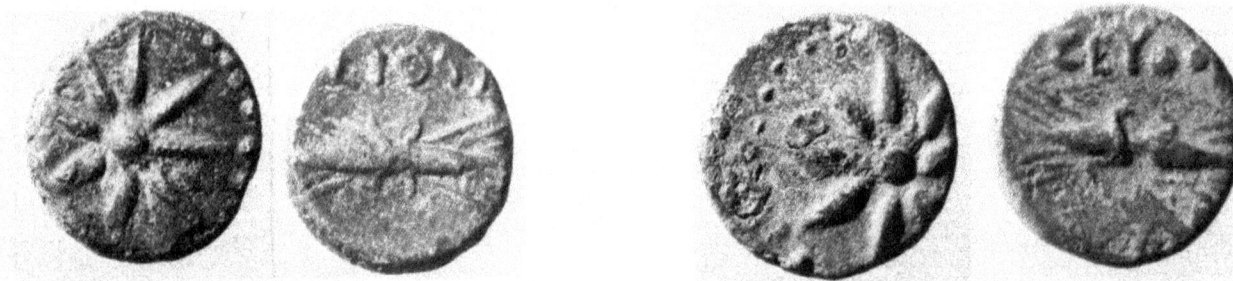

c

d

Fig. 67. Bronze coins minted by Seuthes III (three times magnified)
a. type 1; b. type 2; c. type 3; d. type 4.

Fig. 68. Bronze coins minted by Seuthes III, type 5 (three times magnified)

Fig. 69. Bronze coins minted by Seuthes III, type 6 (three times magnified)

Fig. 70. Bronze coins minted by Seuthes III, type 7 (three times magnified)

Fig. 71.   Greek inscription found in the Sanctuary of the Palace

Fig. 72. The stone bases on the agora

Fig. 73. The base with an inscription

Fig. 74.   Altar-hearth from the Sanctuary in the Palace

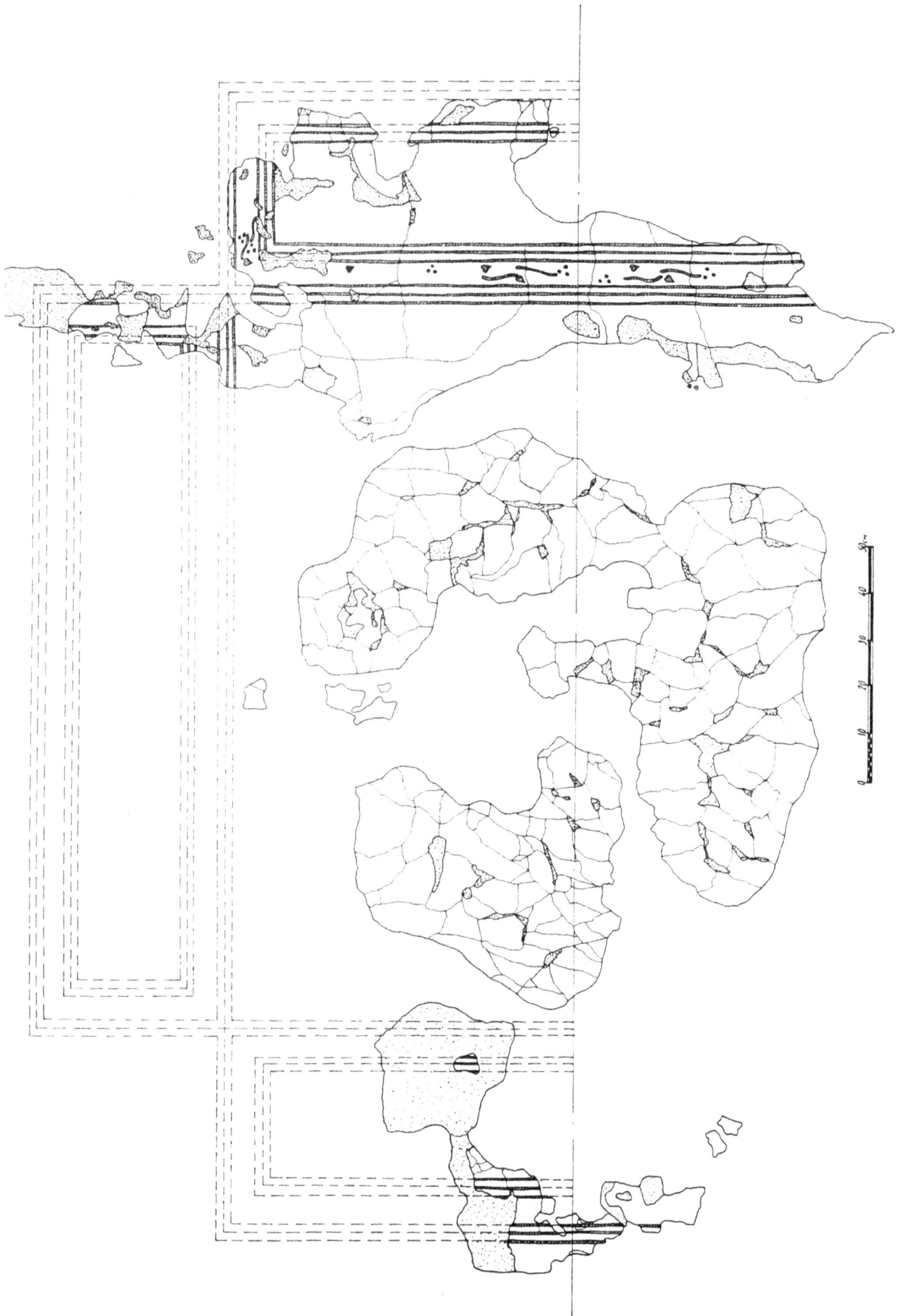

Fig. 75   The hearth in the throne room.

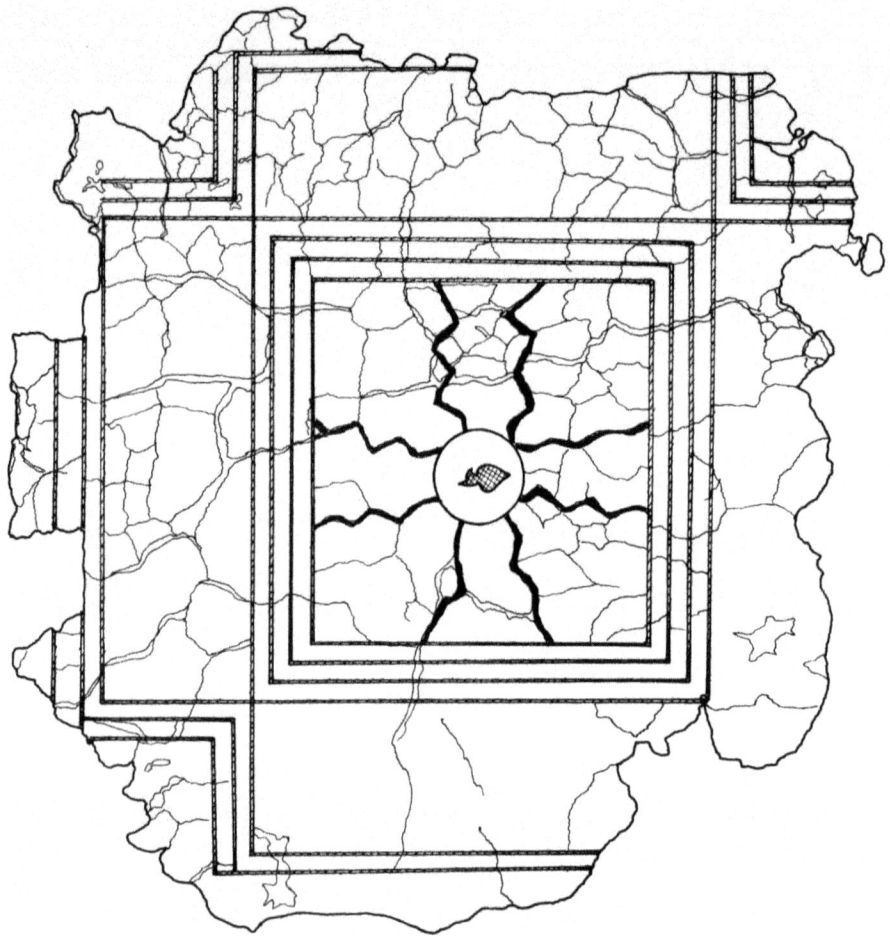

Fig. 76. Altar-hearth ornamented with thunderbolts

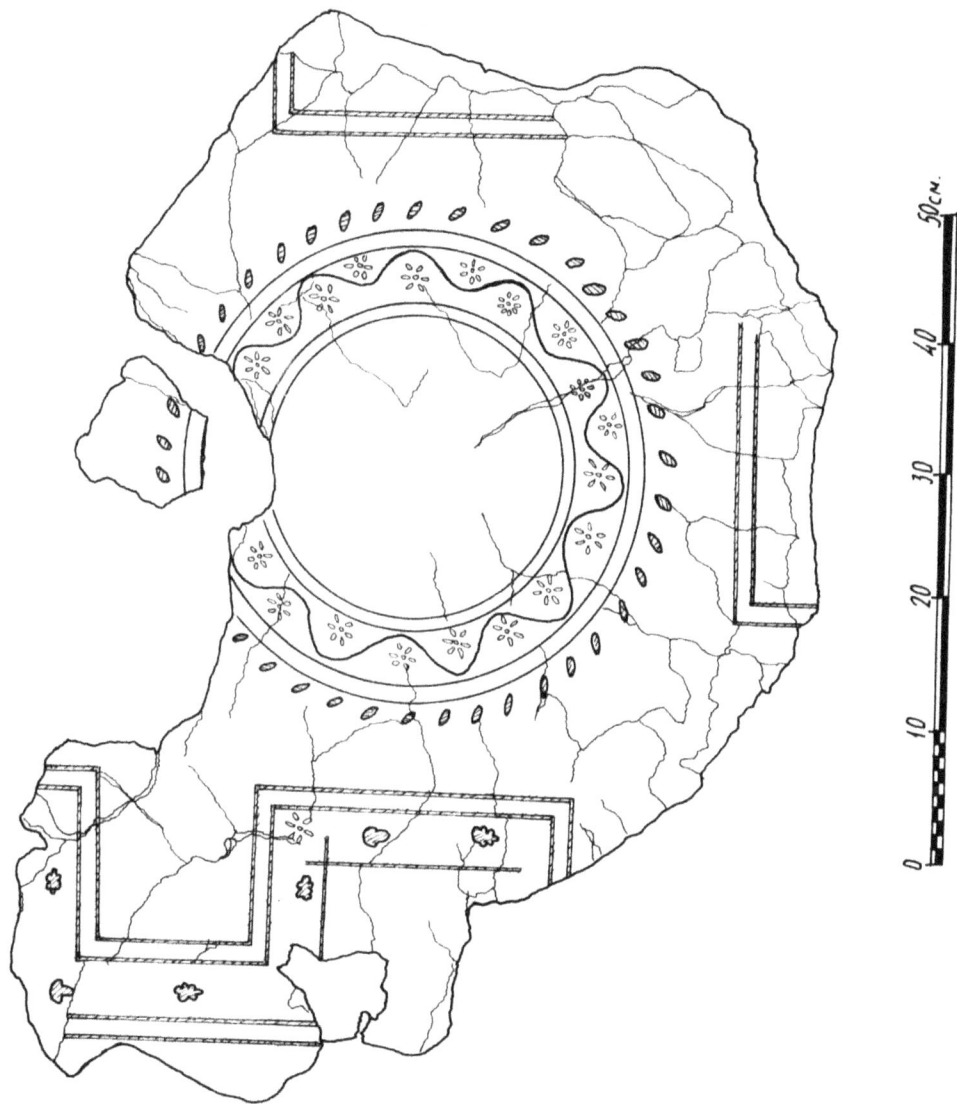

Fig. 77. Altar-hearth with a garland of rosettes

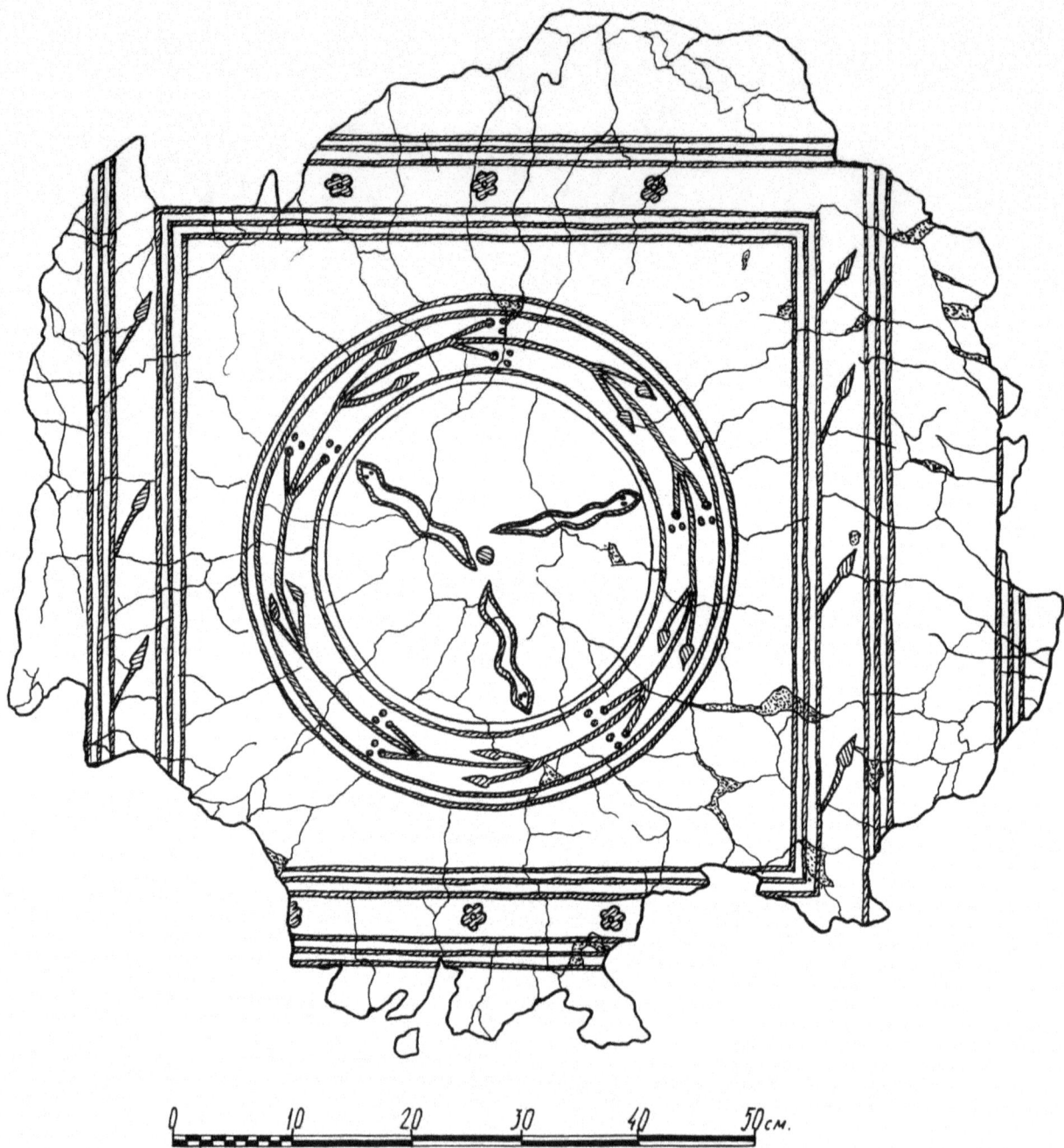

Fig. 78. Altar-hearth with an ornament composed of three snakes

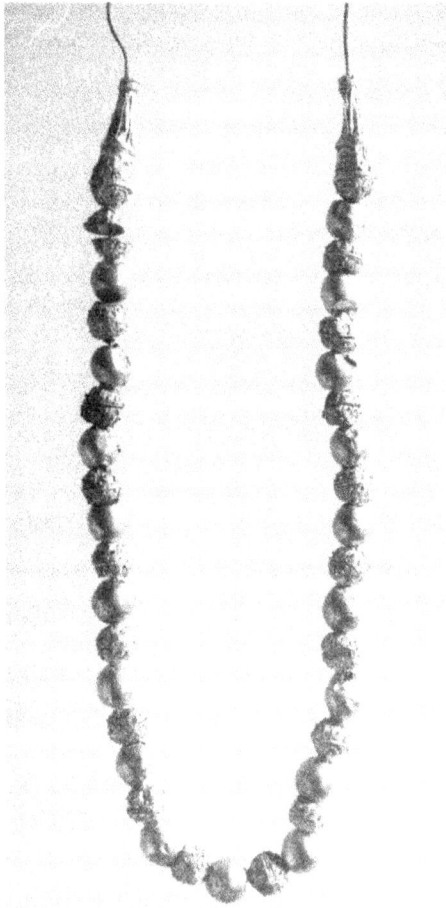

Fig. 79. Gold necklace from tumulus No. 1

Fig. 80. Gold earrings ending in a lion's head from tumulus No. 1

Fig. 81. Bronze oinochoe from tumulus No. 1

Fig. 82. Bronze situla from tumulus No. 1 - detail

Fig. 83. Terracotta figurine of a woman from tumulus No. 1

Fig. 84.   Discovery of the beehive tomb in tumulus No. 2

Fig. 85.   Beehive tomb from tumulus No. 2, seen from the North

Fig. 87.   Brick tomb No. 3 in tumulus No. 2, seen from the South-west

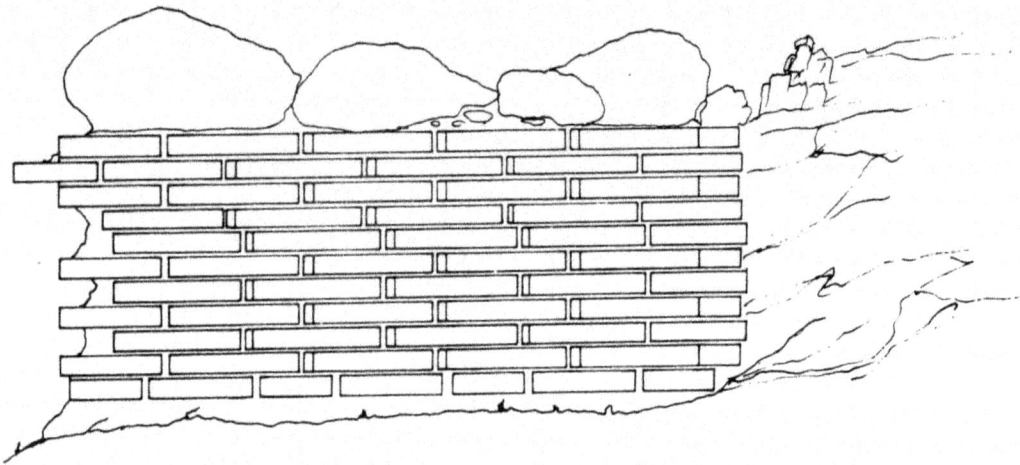

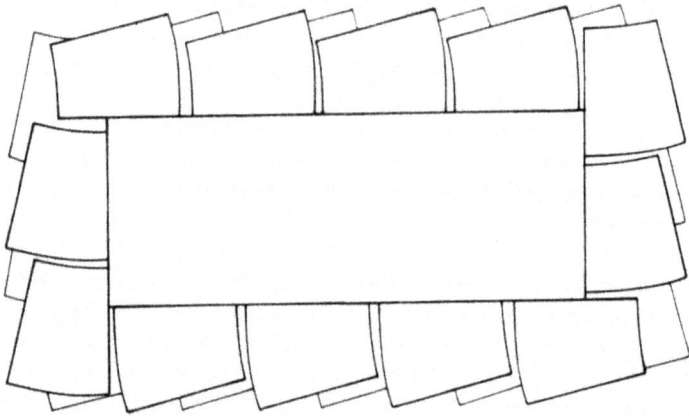

Fig. 86   Brick construction in tomb no. 2.

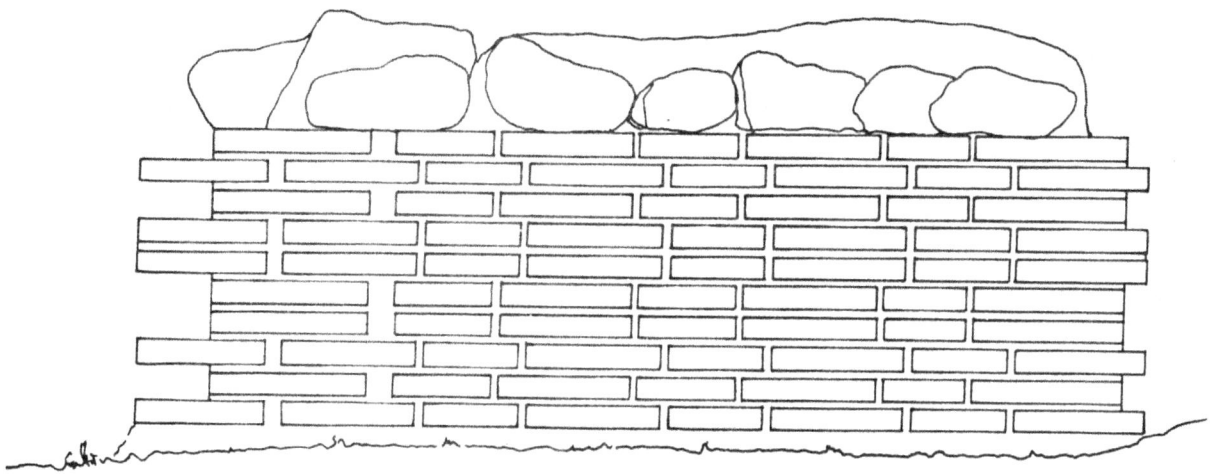

Fig. 89   Brick construction in tomb no. 3.

Fig. 88. Brick tomb No. 3 in tumulus No. 2, seen from the South-west

Fig. 90. Gold necklace from tomb No. 2 in tumulus No. 2

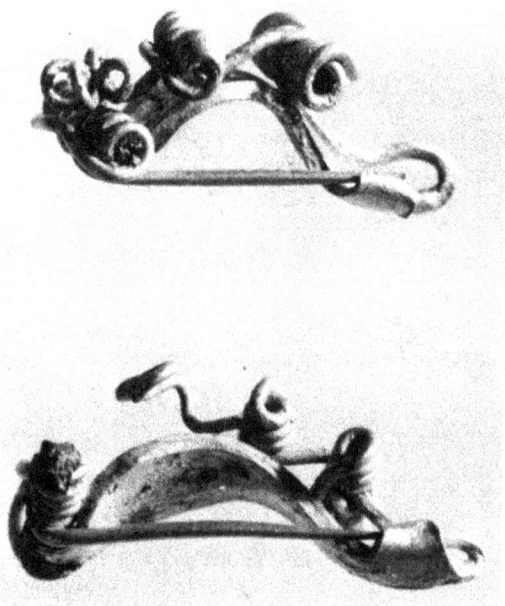

Fig. 91. Gold fibulae from tomb No. 2 in tumulus No. 2

Fig. 92. Little gold plaque with the head of a young man from tomb No. 2

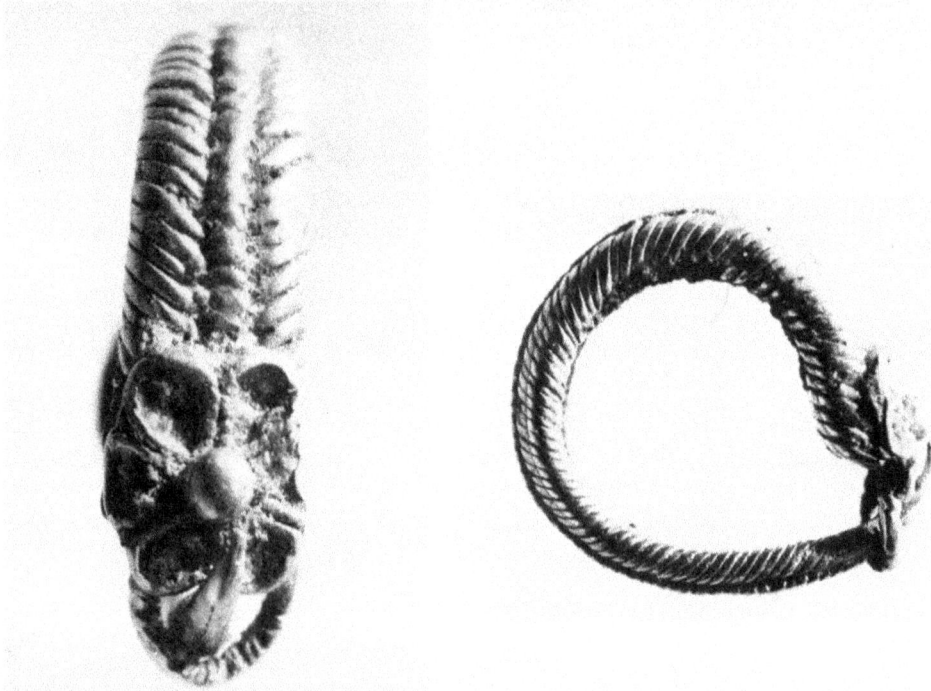

Fig. 93. Gold earring from tomb No. 3 in tumulus No. 2

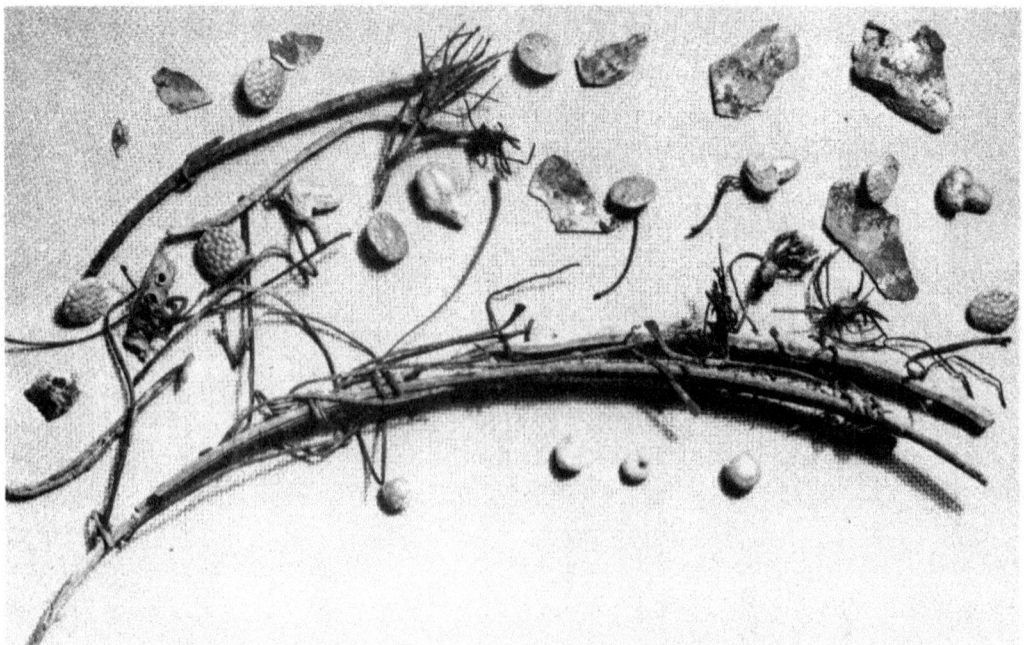

Fig. 94. Parts of a burial wreath from tomb No. 3

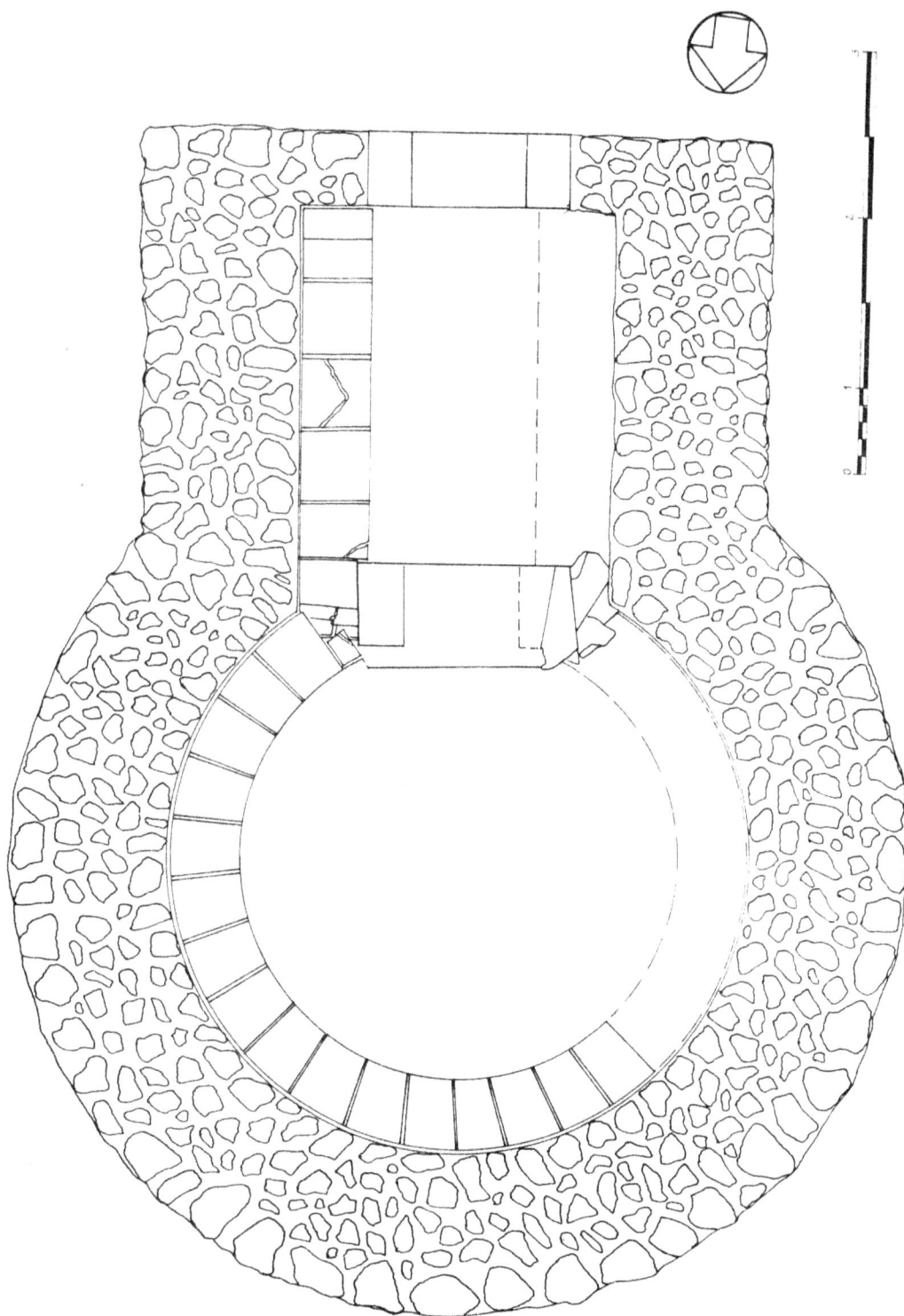

Fig. 95. Plan of beehive tomb in tumulus no. 3.

Fig. 96. Beehive tomb from tumulus No. 3, viewed from the South-west

Fig. 97. Beehive tomb from tumulus No. 3, viewed from the North-west

Fig. 98. Beehive tomb from tumulus No. 3 after the stone covering was removed